Best ▪ Hikes With

CH▲LDREN™

in Western Washington & the Cascades

VOLUME 2

Best Hikes With
CHILDREN™

in Western Washington
& the Cascades

VOLUME 2

By Joan Burton

Photographs by
Bob and Ira Spring

The Mountaineers

5 4 3 2
5 4 3 2 1

Published by The Mountaineers
1011 SW Klickitat Way, Seattle, Washington 98134

Published simultaneously in Canada by Douglas & McIntyre, Ltd., 1615 Venables Street, Vancouver, B.C. V5L 2H1

Published simultaneously in Great Britain by Cordee, 3a DeMontfort Street, Leicester, England, LE1 7HD

Manufactured in the United States of America

Edited by Miriam Bulmer
Maps by Debbie Newell
All photographs by Bob & Ira Spring except: pages 2, 59, 61, 62 by Kirkendall/Spring; pages 41, 92, 104, 130, 133, 135 by John Spring
Cover design by Elizabeth Watson
Book layout by Connie Bollen
Typography by Graphics West

Cover photograph: Summit of Clear West Peak; photo by Kirkendall/Spring
Frontispiece: Two-year-old Lisa Ritland

Library of Congress Cataloging in Publication Data
Burton, Joan, 1935–
   Best hikes with children in western Washington & the Cascades.

   Includes index.
   1. Hiking—Washington (State)—Guidebooks.   2. Mountaineering—Cascade Range—Guidebooks.   3. Family recreation—Northwest, Pacific—Guidebooks.   4. Children—Travel—Northwest, Pacific—
Guidebooks.   I. Spring, Bob, 1918–   II. Spring, Ira.   III. Title.
GV199.42.W2B87   1988   917'.97   88-23463
ISBN 0-89886-179-9 (v. 1)
ISBN 0-89886-334-1 (v. 2)

Contents

Driftwood on Spencer Spit

Introduction

To children, all the natural world is a place of wonder. Not a creature or phenomenon is taken for granted. Yet along with curiosity, children may feel fear and dread and other restraints; they may not trust their surroundings enough to risk the delight and joy of exploring. Moreover their span of attention is short; many things call to them at once. How can parents capture the child's attention and thereby enrich his sense of wonder? Focus. Enter your children's perceptions at their own level and time scale. Have you ever looked at "bellyflowers" with a child? In dry alpine areas many flowers grow only two or three inches tall. By lying on your belly, you can really see them through the eyes of a child. Focus intensely with the child on the color, form, and design of each tiny plant and blossom. What flowers or other objects in his or her previous experience do they resemble? Use all the senses. Absorb all the wonder of those tiny blossoms.

Explore. Be curious. Question, examine, observe. In a warm pond with a mud bottom you can find myriad tiny creatures. Look for pollywogs, lizards, newts, helgrammites, skippers, water boatmen, and dragonflies. Children don't need to know their Latin names, about evolutionary processes, or about the food chain. Let time stand still while they look and wonder about living, moving creatures. The delight in their swimming, skimming, flying, and landings can be more than enough.

A nurse log and its decaying upturned stump can be sources of wonder to children. Have them examine the dead wood for tiny new trees germinating in the log. All manner of ferns, mosses, and bushes start life more readily in the warmer temperatures of an old log than in the surrounding soil. The contorted roots of the upended stump can inspire young imaginations. Perhaps they can see a throne, a cave, or a castle battlement in the twisted shapes, or imagine elves and gnomes hiding between the roots. Children familiar with *The Hobbit*, *The Wind in the Willows*, or *The Lion, The Witch and The Wardrobe* can project the characters of these works into such a setting.

Children may be frightened, at first, at the roar and scope and scale of an ocean beach. Yet the surf has a magnetic quality for them. A parent can explain that the power and possible danger of the ocean waves needs to be respected, while sharing the joy and excitement of the pounding waves, the wonder of tide flats and tide pools, clam holes, driftwood, seaweed, and shorebirds. Once a breaker has crashed, its surging foam rushes in, then recedes. Children love to play tag with the miniature wave, guessing how close it will come to them without washing over their feet, then racing away in the nick of time.

You can catch a glimpse of the magic of the universe while marveling at an avalanche lily in bloom, cradling a frog, or gazing at the Milky Way on a dark summer night. There is wonder in all of these—clear, astonished wonder at the why and the how and the if of the world. As far as we know, the wonder has not changed from the beginning of human history. It is the subtle driving force that for centuries has pointed curious minds toward the sciences and the quest to know. But the basic drive that starts our wonder, the glimpse through a slightly opened door, can be stopped by an avalanche of facts and figures, theorems, laws, and equations. Too much information given too soon can snuff out the spark of wonder. Children need only to sample, question, and be intrigued by what they see in the natural world. Let them seek out their own answers.

HIKING WITH CHILDREN

Since my first book came out, I have heard from parents that some hikes turned out to be more challenging, and harder work, than they expected. Were my children super athletes? Did they never whine, or was I immune to whining, tears, and long uphill grinds? How could I have made those hikes sound so easy and rewarding?

Of course, hindsight does filter out sweat, tears, and long switchbacks. But I have to repeat my message. My kids hiked because they had fun. They didn't have fun at every step, but they did love the taste of adventure hiking brought them. I believe they even enjoyed testing themselves. Certainly they enjoyed competing with one another on trails. So my answer is still yes, hiking with kids was and can be fun and rewarding for both the children and the parents.

Though each parent comes up with his or her own variations on the theme of motivation, here are some of the strategies that worked with my children when they were young, susceptible, and believed everything I told them.

1. Appoint a "First Leader." I rotated this official designation among my three children. Somehow, being tagged "First Leader" imparted status—and extra energy, at least for a while. Unspoken competition between brothers and sisters can be a powerful motivating force (which is why we did not encourage walking sticks). It's a good idea to agree in advance on a point at which the official title rotates again.

2. Frequent "energy stops." As in, "When we get to that creek ahead, we'll need to have an energy stop, where we'll have some..."

3. "Energy food." Candy, fruit, or a favorite family treat. Never called candy, and always rationed out in tiny increments to prolong its effectiveness.

4. Take a friend along. Aches, pains, and complaints are often forgotten when there is a companion the child's own age along on the

Four-year-old Erik Spring on Clear West Peak

hike. The child will not want to look slow or tired in front of the friend, and a little friendly rivalry, not unlike sibling rivalry, won't hurt.

5. Praise, praise, praise. Only the parent knows how thick to spread this, but positive reinforcement may have the most durable results of all. When my sister and I were eight and nine, my father took us to Melakwa Lake. More than forty years later I still remember what a fuss he made over how strong and fast we were. His praise was probably vast exaggeration, but consider the effect it had.

6. Patience. This means taking time, if necessary, to inspect every creek, throw sticks and stones over bridges, look up for birds, and down at animal tracks. If parents want to get home (or into a camp-site) before dark, they must plan ahead for a pace to fit the child's ability and attention span. Try not to look at your watch any more than necessary. If you keep winding it and shaking it, the child will suspect you are not having as much fun as he or she is.

HOW TO USE THIS BOOK

As in my last book, most of the hikes described in this guidebook are in the Cascade Range or the Olympic Mountains. A few are found in nearby foothills and lowlands. New areas include Lake Chelan, the San Juans, and the Long Beach area.

Each hike description includes (1) a block summarizing important information about each hike, (2) symbols for features of special interest, and (3) the description itself, which tells you what to expect, how to get to the trail, and where to go from there.

Hikes are rated *easy*, *moderate*, or *difficult* for children. These ratings are only approximations. I tried to factor in distance, elevation gain, and trail condition, but even those are not altogether objective criteria. I thought of giving minimum age levels for trails, but found that to be even more subjective. A trail one five-year-old is capable of hiking may be too difficult for another. In any case, the most important factor is motivation. If kids want to hike somewhere, energy and stamina will follow. The reverse is also true: if children do not want to go on, any trail at any time can be too steep and too long.

The great majority of hikes can be completed in one day, but camping opportunities are plentiful and have been noted for families who are more adventurous or experienced. Some trips are primarily overnight excursions, but beginning sections can make good dayhikes; it is not always necessary to walk the entire distance.

In the same way, many hikes that are rated *moderate* or *difficult* contain shorter, easier sections that make excellent dayhikes in their own right. So if you want a shorter outing, don't restrict your search to only those hikes that I have rated *easy*. Instead, scan the more difficult trips for what I call "turnarounds," which are marked in the margin by a special symbol (see "Key to Symbols" below). Turnarounds are satisfying destinations that make fine picnic spots and feature scenic views or other natural attractions. You can turn around at a turnaround and feel well satisfied with your hike.

I have also indicated the months during which each trail is free of snow. This can vary from year to year. Early or late in the season, when there may be some doubt about current snow conditions, call the local ranger station in the area where you want to hike.

Hikers venturing into wild or otherwise roadless areas should carry an agency area map and compass (most outdoor-equipment stores stock them) and know how to use them. Custom Correct, Green Trails, U.S. Forest Service, and/or National Park Service maps are listed for each hike.

Maps

Though the maps included in this book are fine for an overall view of the hike's location and major landmarks, they are no substitute for official agency topographic maps. United States Geologic Survey (U.S.G.S.) maps are being updated but do not always have current road or trail numbers. I have tried to make current information available in the hike descriptions. The numbering of National Forest roads has become rather complicated. Major forest roads are identified by two-

or four-digit numbers, but those designating minor roads may have seven digits. In such numbers the first three digits indicate the main road, the remainder, a particular spur leading off the main one. Be sure the map you carry is as up to date as possible.

Road mileage is expressed in decimals rounded to the nearest tenth of a mile. Trail mileage is expressed in fractions and all mileages are as accurate as possible.

WHAT TO TAKE

Boots

Rocky, uneven trails can subject small feet and shoes alike to more wear and tear than they are designed to handle. On many of the shorter, gentler trails in this book, running shoes or other sneakers may be adequate, but on longer, steeper trails, or when carrying a heavy pack, such footwear may not offer enough protection. Boots are a must for extended dayhikes and all backpack trips. Unfortunately, boots for children are expensive—especially since children's feet somehow seem to grow even faster than the rest of them. But there's hope for the budget. I bought one pair of good boots for the first child, passed them down the line, and traded around outgrown hand-me-downs with other families. Some outdoor-equipment stores will take back usable children's boots for their rental trade and offer a price based on their value, which can be applied to the next pair.

In buying boots (for children or adults), keep in mind that boots that don't fit properly can make their owner utterly miserable. (So can wet tennis shoes.) It is therefore important to make sure your child's boots fit properly. They should be snug enough to prevent chafing but not so tight that they pinch toes. After buying your child a pair of boots, have him or her wear them inside the house for several days before using them outdoors. This will not only help to break in the boots but will often reveal poorly fitting ones while it's still possible to return them. Usually, an ill-fitting pair can be returned for full value. Even well-fitting boots, however, need to be broken in before they are suitable for an extended hike. Otherwise, blisters are virtually certain. For that reason, children forced to hike far in stiff new boots may never willingly hike anywhere again.

Packs

Child-size packs and bags are available at most backpacking stores, but parents can calculate how soon they will be outgrown and how much use they will get. Sometimes, packs are a source of rivalry among little children, who are likely to gauge another child's load by size alone. Unless a child has his or her own pack, a good parental strategy is to fill an adult daypack with the child's extra clothing, take a tuck in the straps, and allow him or her to appear to be carrying an enormous load. This is a sure-fire morale booster for a kid. Other children on the trail are not likely to heft one another's packs, so no one but the parents will know how much is in it.

The Ten Essentials

Over the years, The Mountaineers has compiled a list of ten items that should be taken on every hike. These "Ten Essentials" not only make your trip more comfortable, but equip you to cope with emergencies caused by bad weather, injury, or other unforeseen circumstances.

1. Extra clothing. Weather changes or an unplanned swim mean trouble if there are no changes of clothing.

2. Extra food. Carry enough food so that if your hike lasts longer than you expect, you and your children won't be hungry.

3. Sunglasses. Bright sun on snow or water can be blinding.

4. Knife. Useful in countless situations.

5. Firestarter-candle or chemical fuel. If you should unexpectedly have to stay overnight, you will want to build a fire.

6. First-aid kit. Keep it well supplied and hope you won't need to use it.

7. Matches in a waterproof container. No fire is possible without them. Look for waterproof matches in outing stores.

8. Flashlight. Imagine walking down a trail in the dark with little children—without a light.

9. Map. Be sure that you have the correct and current map for your hike.

10. Compass. Know how to use it with your map to orient yourself in the field.

Children require a few extra essentials; the items mentioned below are ones I found useful.

Mosquitoes, no-see-ums, gnats, deerflies, and sunburn can make anyone miserable. Obviously you will need protection from insects and sun. But chemical products designed for adult skin—particularly sunscreens with high SPFs—may be too harsh for children. Take the time to test untried products before you leave home. Don't assume they will be safe if there is even a possibility of an allergic reaction—two miles away from the car and fifty miles from home is no place to find out.

Be sure each child has a long-sleeved shirt to wear when bugs attack. There may even be times when a cap, gloves, and long pants will be needed. Repellent helps some but is overrated. Give the kids (and yourselves) personal "habitats"—a six-foot length of no-see-um netting for each camper, light enough to wad up in a pocket, large enough to cover the head and be tucked under the bottom at dinner time. If your child is allergic to bee or wasp stings, be sure to carry the appropriate medications prescribed or recommended by your physician.

Your first-aid kit should also contain any other special medicines or supplies your child may need, such as extra moleskin for blisters on tender feet, extra toilet paper, and some baking soda to plaster on nettle or other stings.

Do not encourage children to go into lakes in jeans, because wet jeans can become extremely cold and uncomfortable later when walking out. Carry shorts or bathing suits for wading and swimming. Also, hidden hazards lie on lake bottoms. Carry an extra pair of tennis shoes for the child to wade in, to protect him or her from sharp rocks and sticks buried in muddy lake bottoms.

Food

Food is a matter of family preference, of course. My family enjoyed meals whose ingredients came from the grocery store rather than those with freeze-dried foods from sporting goods stores. Freeze-dried foods are not only more expensive, but also less tasty than familiar home favorites. Don't experiment with unknown, gourmet foods on a camping trip with children. Comfort foods are one-pot meals—such as stew, chili, chicken and noodles, etc.—that children know from home. Dayhike foods should be combinations of nuts, fruit, candies, raisins, cheese, and crackers that are easy to carry without being crushed in the pack, and impart energy.

Safety

Backcountry travel, even on dayhikes, entails unavoidable risks that every hiker assumes and must be aware of and respect. The fact that a trail is described in this book is not a representation that it will be safe for you. The trips presented here vary in difficulty and in the amount and kind of preparation needed to enjoy them safely. Some routes may have changed, or conditions on them may have deteriorated since this book was written. Also, of course, especially in mountain areas, conditions can change even from day to day, owing to weather and other factors. A trip that is safe in good weather or for a well-conditioned, properly equipped hiker may be completely unsafe for someone else, or unsafe for anyone in adverse weather.

You can minimize your risks by being knowledgeable, prepared, and alert. There is not space in this book for a general treatise on wilderness safety, but there are a number of good books and public courses on the subject, and you should take advantage of them to increase your knowledge. Just as important, you should always be aware of your limitations and the conditions existing when and where you are traveling. If conditions are dangerous, or if you are not pre-

Mount Shuksan and cairn on Table Mountain

pared to deal with them safely, change your plans! It is better to have wasted a few days than to be the subject of a wilderness rescue.

These warnings are not intended to keep you out of the wilderness. Most people enjoy safe trips through the backcountry every year. However, one element of the beauty, freedom, and excitement of the wilderness is the presence of risks that do not confront us at home. When you travel in the backcountry, you assume those risks. They can be met safely, but only if you exercise your own independent good judgment and common sense.

Water

Drinking water is another cause for concern and preparation. Do not assume that streams and lakes will supply you with pure water. Most mountain water is safe, but much is not, and there's no way to tell. If the trail is popular and the lake is crowded, be suspicious. Carry a canteen or plastic bottle of water or flavored drinks for the trail. (If you carry in cans of juice or pop, be sure to carry out the empties.) Cooking water must be boiled at least twenty minutes. Iodine tablets or water filtering devices also guarantee pure water.

Hypothermia

Most of the mountain lakes described here are very cold, and weather conditions in the mountains can change abruptly. Parents should be aware of the hazards of hypothermia and carry extra clothing, and perhaps a thermos of cocoa or hot soup. Because of their relatively small body size, little children are vulnerable to hypothermia sooner than adults exposed to the same conditions. In fact, a parent may not even recognize the symptoms in children. Children with first-stage hypothermia can be listless, whiny, and unwilling to cooperate, long before physical signs, like shivering, start to appear. Since these symptoms can also occur on hikes when children are only tired, bored, or hungry, it is important to rule out hypothermia before assuming some other cause. Early morning, late afternoon and evening, and periods of cool, overcast weather are times to be particularly alert to your child's behavior and to take immediate steps to rewarm him or her if appropriate.

GOOD OUTDOOR MANNERS

Hiking families have an obligation to teach children good outdoor manners. The hiker's motto should be "Leave trails and campsites as clean or cleaner than you found them." Parents can set an example by cleaning up someone else's messy camp and carrying out or burning leftover trash. Do not leave old plastic tarps behind for the next camping family. They blow around, are quickly ripped and tattered, and add to the litter. In fact, anything you can carry in, you can carry out. Think about how your family feels at seeing old tin cans, bottles, and plastic containers in places they have hiked miles to see.

Tell children they must not drop candy or gum wrappers, orange peels, or peanut or egg shells. These things take a long time to break down, and petrified orange peels are not an archaeological find we want to leave to posterity. Also, don't bury garbage; it doesn't stay covered for long.

Carry out cans, aluminum foil, and disposable diapers. One way to handle such materials in parents' packs is to include several zippable plastic bags for garbage, wet clothing, and the things children find along the way that they want to bring home.

Teach your children to dispose of toilet paper properly. Burying it with their stools used to be acceptable, but little creatures dig up the paper and strew it about. I've seen campsites so littered with toilet paper, the prospect of camping there was disgusting. If your family has a campsite, burn toilet paper or put it in plastic bags and pack it out. Parents should check their children's toilet area after use, to be sure they have the technique down and the area is usable by the next visitors.

How do you teach children to care about the environment? To conserve, value, and care for that which cannot be replaced? The obvious answer: by parental example.

Offering an option rather than forbidding certain behavior usually works best. Instead of allowing your daughter to strip flowers along the trail for a bouquet, suggest taking a close-up picture of one, or getting down on hands and knees to examine the tiny petals. Carry binoculars for observing distant soaring birds. Suggest looking closely at starfish and anemones, but leaving them on their rocks to gather food at the next tide. If children turn over rocks to look for crabs and snails, offer to help them put the rocks back in place, so the creatures' homes are intact. If children want to collect living tree fungus and mushrooms, suggest they leave them growing, and instead look for fir, cedar, and hemlock cones.

Once, while we were camping in an ocean-side rain forest park, we came across children who were stripping thick cushions of moss from old trees for their mattresses. My family was thunderstruck. We realized they didn't know any better, so we remonstrated, "Don't do that. The moss took a long time to grow." The other children didn't care, and we had no authority to stop them.

I later told our children that those in the rain forest who were stripping the trees of their moss were beginners, who displayed their ignorance by their behavior. No one likes to feel like an ignorant amateur.

What about pets? Dogs are permitted, but not welcomed, on national forest trails. They are absolutely not allowed in national parks. Though children may love dayhiking with their pet, its presence in a backpacking campsite may impact birds and small animals and annoy other campers, who came partly to get away from domestic animals.

You should know that theft, both in camps and from parked cars

Fun on a summer snowbank

at trailheads, has become a major problem. So many hikers' cars have been vandalized that wise hikers arrange to be dropped off and picked up from trailheads. If you must leave a parked car for several days, don't tempt thieves by leaving expensive clothing and gear in plain view. Tell a Forest Service official, if you can, that you will be parked at such-and-such a trailhead for a duration of time, and you would appreciate having someone check your car during patrols of the area.

A NOTE ABOUT SAFETY

Safety is an important concern in all outdoor activities. No guidebook can alert you to every hazard or anticipate the limitations of every reader. Therefore, the descriptions of roads, trails, routes, and natural features in this book are not representations that a particular place or excursion will be safe for your party. When you follow any of the routes described in this book, you assume responsibility for your own safety. Under normal conditions, such excursions require the usual attention to traffic, road and trail conditions, weather, terrain, the capabilities of your party, and other factors. Keeping informed on current conditions and exercising common sense are the keys to a safe, enjoyable outing.

LEGEND

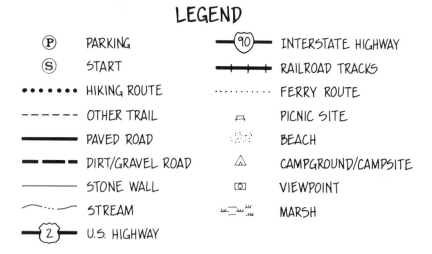

KEY TO SYMBOLS

 Dayhikes. These are hikes that can be completed in a single day. While some trips allow camping, only a few require it.

 Backpack trips. These are hikes whose length or difficulty makes camping out either necessary or recommended for most families.

 Easy trails. These are relatively short, smooth, gentle trails suitable for small children or first-time hikers.

 Moderate trails. Most of these are 2 to 4 miles total distance and feature more than 500 feet of elevation gain. The trail may be rough and uneven. Hikers should wear lug-soled boots and be sure to carry the Ten Essentials.

 Difficult trails. These are often rough, with considerable elevation gain or distance to travel. They are suitable for older or experienced children. Lug-soled boots and the Ten Essentials are standard equipment.

 Hikable. The best times of year to hike each trail are indicated by the following symbols: flower—spring; sun—summer; leaf—fall; snowflake—winter.

 Driving directions. These paragraphs tell you how to get to the trailheads.

 Turnarounds. These are places, mostly along moderate trails, where families can cut their hike short yet still have a satisfying outing. Turnarounds usually offer picnic opportunities, views, or special natural attractions.

 Cautions. These mark potential hazards—cliffs, stream or highway crossing, and the like—where close supervision of children is strongly recommended.

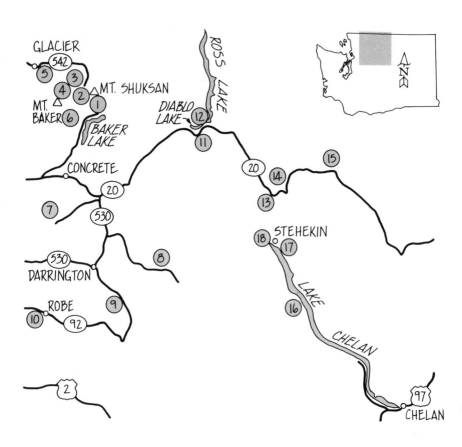

Mount Baker and the North Cascades

Mount Shuksan from Artists Ridge Trail

1. Artists Ridge

Type:	Dayhike
Difficulty:	Easy for children
Hikable:	Late July–September
One way:	¹/₂ mile loop
High point:	5200 feet
Elevation gain and loss:	200 feet
Green Trails map:	No. 14 Mt. Shuksan
U.S. Forest Service map:	Mt. Baker–Snoqualmie

A short, gentle paved loop leads to kid-size, heather-framed tarns (small lakes sculpted in bedrock by a passing glacier) and summer snowbanks, dramatic views of Mount Baker and Mount Shuksan, and lessons in volcano behavior. Signs along the way give explanatory geological information in terms kids can understand, about the formation of Mount Shuksan and Mount Baker. The trail ends a few feet from the top of Artists Ridge. For those with very young children or those intimidated by the steep Table Mountain trail (Hike 2), this makes a picturesque short alternative.

From Bellingham, drive east on Mount Baker Highway 542 through the towns of Deming and Glacier, and in 54 miles reach Heather

Meadows. Go another 2.5 miles to the road end at Kulshan Ridge, the area's official name. (The U.S. Forest Service uses the popular names Artists Point and Artists Ridge.) Find the trailhead on the east side of the parking lot near the restroom (elevation 5100 feet).

Begin alongside summer snowbanks. The first interpretive signs explain Mount Baker's hidden volcanic core in child-appealing language: "The dragon with a fire in its belly." Like all dormant volcanoes in the Northwest, Mount Baker could erupt again at any time. Its most recent activity was in 1976, when it began to emit clouds of steam and ash, giving the Forest Service enough of a scare that they closed Baker Lake's campgrounds for a time. At the top climbers still can smell sulfur in the hot volcanic breath of the dragon, waiting and thinking about breathing his fire again.

Signs also explain the formation of Mount Shuksan, the yellow band of rocks on Shuksan Arm, and the fragile alpine environment. Look the opposite direction at Mount Shuksan's enormous hanging glaciers hundreds of feet thick. Like waterfalls of ice, they flow over rock, break, and crash with avalanche thunder.

The Artists Ridge Trail mounts small knolls crested with heather. In August kids can look for ripe blueberries and huckleberries. Ponds and tarns of snowmelt water warmed by the summer sun make wonderful wading pools. What more can children ask for? The last and largest pool is the prettiest one for capturing the breath-taking views in reflection. Get here early on a clear day for an undisturbed image. At the end of the ridge the trail loops back to the parking lot.

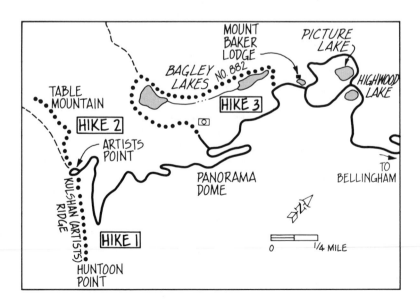

2. Table Mountain

Type: Dayhike
Difficulty: Moderate for children
Hikable: Late July–October
One way: ³/₄ mile to summit,
1¹/₂ mile traverse to connect
with Chain Lakes Trail
High point: 5553 feet
Elevation gain: 600 feet
Green Trails map: No. 14 Mt. Shuksan
U.S. Forest Service map: Mt. Baker–Snoqualmie

An exciting, steep, and very short exposed trail leads to a broad summit plateau between Mount Baker and Mount Shuksan. We carried one of our babies in a backpack to the top when she was less than a year old, and I met a father leading a four-year-old who had also been carried there in a pack, but was walking it for the first time. I overheard a small girl on her way up the cliffs ask, "Mother, how are we ever going to get down?" The trail may not scare all children, but it does frighten some parents, who find it alarmingly exposed. Parental guidance is needed. Although hundreds of families climb Table Mountain every year, if you are not comfortable on the trail, don't take your children. There are other trails. But rest assured, the blasted rock inclines are wide and gentle. Arriving at the summit cairns rewards children with a sense of achievement and satisfaction. Sometimes this trail does not thaw out until mid-August, and some years not at all. Do not attempt it until the snow is gone from the cliffs.

 From Bellingham, drive east on Mount Baker Highway 542 for 54 miles to Heather Meadows. Continue for 2.5 miles to the road end as described for Artists Ridge (Hike 1). Find the trail on the west (right) side of the parking lot (elevation 5100 feet). Do not confuse it with the Chain Lakes Trail.

The Table Mountain Trail was rebuilt in 1987 by crews who blasted their way up the almost vertical northeast face of Table Mountain. For the first ¹/₂ mile the trail climbs easily around and over knolls, passing a small tarn and distorted ancient alpine trees that will frame views of Mount Shuksan and Mount Baker for your camera. Children may want to stop to check the tadpoles in the snowmelt pond before starting up.

Table Mountain Trail and Mount Baker

In the last ¼ mile the trail turns steep and switchbacks up slabs of the near-vertical cliff. Hold on to your children here. A misstep would be serious. Some of the steps are very big for short-legged hikers. If the trail seems scary now, you should have seen it before it was widened. The sense of accomplishment and bravery children feel as they make their way up the little mountain is wonderful to see. The trail levels abruptly near the top; a few feet more brings children to the cairns at the top.

Look first at magnificent Mount Shuksan, named by the Skagit Indians (the name means "rocky and precipitous"), then back to Mount Baker, named Koma Kulshan, or "white, steep mountain," by the Nooksack Indians. Look down to Bagley Lakes (Hike 3) far below. Table Mountain is part of the volcanic formation left by one of Baker's earlier eruptions. The summit is a mile long, truly a tabletop, with edges that seem to drop off to eternity. A trail marked with cairns (piles of rocks) leads across its broad, snowy rock expanse to a 5742-foot true summit and a descent trail that joins the Chain Lakes Trail. Don't take it. Because it is possible to lose the trail when it crosses snow patches, the traverse is not recommended for young children or inexperienced hikers.

3. Bagley Lakes

Type:	Dayhike
Difficulty:	Easy to moderate for children
Hikable:	Late July–September
One way:	1 mile
High point:	4400 feet
Elevation gain:	250 feet
Green Trails map:	No.14 Mt. Shuksan
U.S. Forest Service map:	Mt. Baker–Snoqualmie

Here are two lakes to throw rocks into, ice-cold water to put toes into, and a year-round snow slope to play on. In early summer Bagley Lakes have the added attraction of skiers careening down and hoping to stop at the water's edge. The two alpine lakes lie in the Heather Meadows Recreation Area. One is a man-made reservoir, the second is a deep cirque under Table Mountain. When the trail has been maintained and the snow is gone, it is easy walking for children, with a dam to walk across.

From Bellingham, drive east on Mount Baker Highway 542 for 54 miles to Heather Meadows. Park in the parking area there.

One can reach the snowfield by one of two routes. The first is the Herman Saddle–Bagley Lakes Trail, opposite the ski lift, which passes both lakes. However, there is a 10-foot section on a cliff along the upper lake where the trail has disappeared; it is scheduled to be repaired in 1994. The other is the nature trail beginning at the Austin Pass Information Center. These two trails could be united to form a 2½-mile loop, once the 10-foot section has been repaired.

For the Herman Saddle–Bagley Lakes Trail, go right into the huge parking lot behind the service buildings near Mount Baker Lodge and find the trail on the left-hand side of the lot (elevation 4300 feet).

The trail descends sharply 60 feet, crosses the dam, and with some ups and downs traverses past lower Bagley Lake to the upper. If the trail across the cliff has been repaired, hike to the snowfield at the head of the lake. If not, stop at a small beach just short of the cliff. Expect wet sections: melting snowbanks keep the trail wet all summer.

For upper Bagley Lake and its snowfield, drive from the ski lift a short mile to the Austin Pass Information Center. Find the wide nature trail descending toward Table Mountain through meadows

Upper Bagley Lake and Table Mountain

covered with heather and blueberries. (We picked a bucketful in early September.) At the nature trail's lowest point, an unmaintained trail descends to the head of the lake, the snowfield, and a shallow beach for wading. This section is always wet due to melting snow. Elevation loss is about 200 feet, which must be regained on your way out.

4. Lunch Box Dome

Type:	Dayhike or overnight
Difficulty:	Difficult for children
Hikable:	Late July–September
One way:	2¼ miles
High point:	5884 feet
Elevation gain:	1600 feet
Green Trails map:	No. 13 Mt. Baker
U.S. Forest Service map:	Mt. Baker–Snoqualmie

Every summer, since long before this book was published, hundreds of parents have carried their little children or lured their older ones with bribes in order to hike the Skyline Divide, a wilderness ridge that stands not only between meadow and glacier, but seemingly also between sky and earth. The area is famous for its wildflower fields and spectacular views.

Fortunately, the best flowers and, some say, the best views are on the first high point, unofficially named Lunch Box Dome. Here children can feel they have conquered a mountain, while parents can

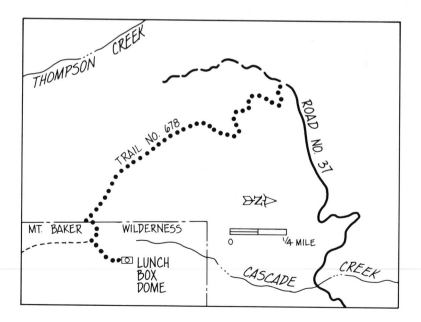

Skyline Divide trail near Lunch Box Dome and Mount Baker

enjoy magnificent views of the two queens of the snow—Baker and Shuksan. Children may also be lucky and see the colony of marmots living in the meadow, and will laugh if one of the fat, clumsy creatures flicks a tail and runs away through the heather.

Drive east from I-5 on Mount Baker Highway 542 to the town of Glacier. One mile beyond the town, turn right on Road No. 39 for 100 feet, then turn left onto Road No. 37 and go 12.7 miles to the trailhead (elevation 4320 feet). Find the Skyline Divide trail No. 678 a few feet up the road from the parking lot.

Begin switchbacking steeply uphill through old-growth firs. Use bribes, promises, candy, and competition to keep the kids moving up the steep part. Expect a few muddy places and lots of roots. Things will look better when meadows begin at 1½ miles. The farther one goes the larger the meadows become, colored in August with blue, white, and yellow—by lupine, valerian, and arnica. At 2 miles, enter the Mount Baker Wilderness. Entering a wilderness area is always a moment to treasure: each one is a monument both to nature and to the countless citizen conservationists who helped preserve these gems. Gasp at the glory of Mount Baker glowing in the sunlight. In ¼ mile more reach the crest of the divide.

Most hikers stop at the ridge top, but the rounded summit of 5884-foot Lunch Box Dome is only a hop, skip, and a jump farther. So, go left up the flower-covered meadow and have a snack in the shade of an alpine fir or mountain hemlock that looks like a Christmas tree. This was a triangulation point used by early surveyors.

Children will be tempted to run and play in the open meadows, but this would be a disaster for the flowers in the thin alpine soil. To keep them busy, open up a Forest Service map and help the children identify the hundreds of peaks to the north and east, and use a road map to figure out the cities to the west, just as the early surveyors did. As the children wolf down their peanut butter sandwiches, contemplate how such a beautiful spot received such a silly name as Lunch Box Dome. The name is not on any map, so who named it? Did a long-ago ranger or fire patrol lose his or her lunch box up here? Or did some tired hikers think it was a good place to eat?

Although the flowers are not as good, and the views are no better, if the children have energy to burn, follow the ups and downs of the Sky Line Ridge Trail southward toward Mount Baker for another mile or so, climbing very steeply up and down some of the highpoints and traversing others. Mount Baker seems so close the children may feel as if they can walk right over onto its glaciers.

5. North Fork Nooksack River

Type: Dayhike
Difficulty: Easy for children
Hikable: March–November
One way: 3 miles
High point: 1050 feet
Elevation gain and loss: 100 feet
Green Trails map: No. 13 Mt. Baker
U.S. Forest Service map: Mt. Baker–Snoqualmie

This river walk is level enough for small children and beautiful enough for any age. This is a great walk anytime, but especially when clouds are low over the ridge tops, Artists Ridge is fogged in, and the wind makes it too miserable to hike the alpine meadows. The rage and volume of the river can hypnotize hiking children into staring fixedly at the angry white water. In late summer occasional sandy beaches appear along the riverbank, but for the most part the river is too deep and swift for wading. Throwing small sticks into the swirling current is allowed.

From Bellingham, drive east on Mount Baker Highway 542 to the town of Glacier, and continue 7 miles to the Wells Creek Road to see Nooksack Falls, right next to the road. Then return west down the highway 5.3 miles to the Douglas Fir Campground (1.8 miles from the Glacier ranger station). Park opposite the campground on the road

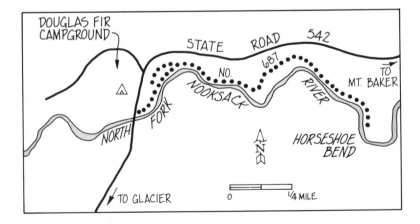

North Fork Nooksack River from trail

shoulder, alongside a bridge at the trailhead (elevation 1000 feet).

Begin on a wide trail at river level next to the voracious Nooksack, which seems to burst out of its bed, chewing at trees and stumps as it passes them. The Nooksack were an Indian tribe who called themselves mountain men. This is their river, fittingly filled with products from those mountains above: mud and glacial silt. The Nooksack has been proposed for designation as a Wild and Scenic River. In a short ¼ mile reach the return part of a loop. Keep right (straight ahead) and cross Coal Creek (dry most of the summer). From here the trail gets a bit rougher. Note how floodwaters have shoved logs along the trail. Overhead, the trail is arched with moss-encrusted vine maples leaning out toward the river. Continue past old cedar stumps on a constructed trail, or go another 1¾ miles on a boot-beaten path to a dead end before returning along the same route. Children can pretend they are Nooksacks tiptoeing along the trail back home to their mountains.

6. Baker Hot Springs

Type: Dayhike
Difficulty: Easy for children
Hikable: May–November
One Way: ¹/₄ mile
High point: 1420 feet
Elevation gain: None
Green Trails map: No. 46 Lake Shannon (trail not shown)
U.S. Forest Service map: Mt. Baker–Snoqualmie

A short easy trail above Baker Lake leads to a popular forest-enclosed hot-springs pool. Parents should be aware that after dark some bathers consider this a suits-optional area. After swimming or

Baker Hot Springs

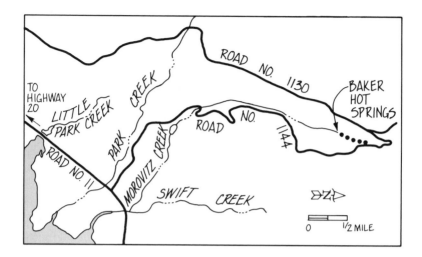

fishing in chilly Baker Lake, however, a warm dip in the hot springs may be so welcome that families might not care. Tell the kids Mount Baker is keeping its furnace heated for their comfort.

Drive east on North Cascades Highway 20. Five miles east of Hamilton, turn north on Baker Lake Road toward Baker Lake. Just beyond Park Creek Campground, near the head of the lake, turn left on Road No. 1144, and after 3.2 miles watch for a parking area on both sides of the road. An unmarked trail at the north end of the parking area leads up a short set of wooden steps. Follow the brief, easy trail east to the hot springs.

The last time Mount Baker erupted, in the 1840s, it destroyed much of its original forest. Some trees around the lake survived the fires and mudflows, and still bear the scars of that eruption. Children can look for charred tree trunks as they start along the hot-springs trail. Mount Baker put on such a thermal show of smoke and ash in the mid-1970s that the Forest Service closed camping on Baker Lake. Since then the volcano has calmed its temper tantrums, but the mountain is still one of the most active of all Cascade volcanoes.

Baker Lake, just below the hot springs, is a popular recreation area, attracting fishermen, boaters, berry pickers, and campers. One of the best swimming sites is off the Shannon Creek Campground. Despite the fact that the lake is really a reservoir, created when Puget Power dammed Baker River in the 1950s, families have enjoyed camping there for generations.

Note: Volunteers keep the hot springs area clean and litter-free, and the Forest Service discourages vandalism and misuse, but hot springs do attract a different crowd. You may wish to check out Baker Hot Springs before taking your children there.

7. Gee Point

Type: Dayhike
Difficulty: Difficult for children
Hikable: July–October
One way: 1¹/₂ miles
High point: 4974 feet
Elevation gain: 700 feet
Green Trails map: No. 77 Oso
U.S. Forest Service map: Mount Baker–Snoqualmie

Gee Point is the site of an abandoned lookout set in the midst of vast replanted clear-cuts in the heart of the North Cascades. The views from the summit are glorious. Kids will love climbing the mountain and looking down to tiny alpine Gee Lake directly below. Why "Gee"? Rather than the exclamation "Gee!", the name may come from the directions given pack animals—"gee" for right and "haw" for left. The trail climbs a very steep hillside. Parents should check this out before letting children loose.

Take Exit 230 from I-5 to North Cascades Highway 20 going east. Just before you reach Concrete, turn right on the Sauk Valley Road. Drive across the Skagit River and turn left, continuing on Sauk Valley Road. Drive 8.7 miles and go right on Road No. 17, the Finney Creek–Cumberland Road. Drive 10.5 miles, then turn right onto Road No. 1720, a rough road. Go 2.0 miles, then turn right onto Road No. 1722,

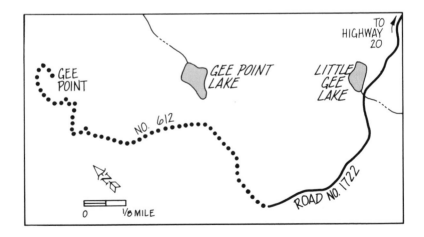

View from old lookout site on Gee Point

a primitive road. Go 2.5 miles to the road's end and the trailhead of Trail No. 612 (elevation 4300 feet).

The trail starts in a clear-cut on a boot-beaten path with rocks, roots, and old stumps: rough for anybody. But in ¼ mile the trail enters woods and some of the misery is over. Pick up the original lookout trail; it is not well maintained, so expect to carry little children at some points, and help older ones over logs and around rocks. At 1 mile the path reaches a level spot and the remains of an old cabin. This is probably as far as the pack train could go. From here the trail has been blasted up a cliff, with switchbacks that reach the summit at 4974 feet. What is the reward for all this? If your kids are like mine, the reward is having a little mountaintop all to yourselves. (Do not expect crowds on this trail. Even Forest Service personnel label it "obscure." Some readers will think there are good reasons for this; others will consider it a challenge.)

On the summit pull out maps and have the kids figure out the names of all the peaks on the skyline. Children will probably want to swim in Gee Point Lake. Unfortunately, you must disappoint them, for there is no trail and the route down is steep and slippery. The panorama of Shuksan, Picketts, Sloan, Whitechuck, Whitehorse, and more is breathtakingly beautiful. Imagine all this range before nineteenth-century homesteaders, miners, and loggers moved in. From this vista, except for the clear-cuts, one can almost imagine it.

8. Buck Creek Campground

Type:	Dayhike or overnight
Difficulty:	Moderate for children
Hikable:	July–September
One way:	2½ miles
High point:	1100 feet
Elevation gain:	250 feet
Green Trails map:	No. 79 Snowking Mountain
U.S. Forest Service map:	Mt. Baker–Snoqualmie Forest

There is some compensation for the possible loss of the spectacular views and flower fields of Green Mountain, which until the massive floods of 1989 was a beautiful dayhike, suitable for children. The Suiattle

Giant boulder in Boulder Creek Campground

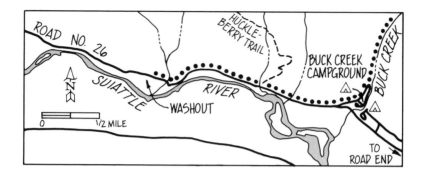

River Road has been changed from a busy, dusty forest road to a pleasant, solitary walk, marred only by an occasional off-road vehicle. The hike ends at a lovely, and formerly popular, Forest Service camp along the banks of noisy, rushing Buck Creek. While this hike is possible most of the year for adults, during periods of high water there is a difficult stream crossing.

Drive State Highway 530 north from Darrington or south from east Rockport. Turn onto the Suiattle River Road No. 26 and drive 12.7 miles to the barricade marking the end of the drivable road (elevation 950 feet).

The Suiattle River took a huge bite out of the road when it changed its course in 1989. Walk the road some 300 feet, and find a trail around the missing section of road. Back on the road again, continue on. At 1 mile is the potentially difficult tributary stream crossing. Windows through the brush open out onto the Suiattle River, giving children glimpses of the current's power and its appetite for chewing up its banks.

At 1¾ miles pass the Huckleberry Mountain trailhead, and at 2¼ miles a sign for Buck Creek Camp, with a spur road leading left up into the campground. Continue on the main road for another ¼ mile to a concrete bridge over the creek. Just before the bridge go left into the campground.

Take your pick of a dozen or more secluded campsites; several are on benches above the river. Those at river level offer backwater pools, riffles, and big boulders for children to play on. Want to do more? At the upper end of the campground, near the creek, find Buck Creek Trail No. 781 and enjoy a short mile of forest. It is said that in the fall salmon spawn here.

9. Beaver Lake

Type: Dayhike
Difficulty: Easy for children
Hikable: March–November
One way: 1½ miles
High point: 1000 feet
Elevation gain: None
Green Trails map: No. 111 Sloan Peak
U.S. Forest Service map: Mt. Baker–Snoqualmie

A beaver colony built itself a luxury layout of dams and underwater condos at the 1½-mile point on this trail, then moved away. The condos were washed out in the floods of 1990, but two dams remain, and by the fall of 1991 a beaver had returned to begin again. Today the creeks flowing into the Sauk River on the Beaver Lake Trail No. 629 have the remains of a series of dams, lakes, pools, and islands that would be the envy of a land-use planner. Children enjoy the engineering feats of beaver loggers and bulldozers. The new beaver is freshening up an existing dam by tucking in branches with green leaves still attached and gnawing on standing alder trees for his lunches and dinners. Rubber boots for little children are recommended because the trail is quite muddy in spots, and kids find boots so satisfying for stomping in. In midsummer expect nettles; children will need long pants and gloves.

Drive I-5 north to Exit 208, then go east on State Highway 530 past Arlington to Darrington. Follow signs for the Mountain Loop

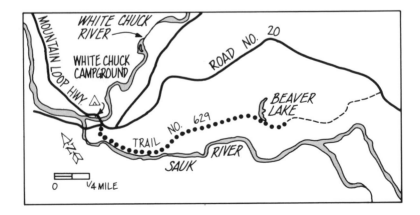

Beaver Lake and old railroad trestle, now a trail

Highway, which becomes Road No. 20. Follow Road No. 20 along the west side of the Sauk River for 10 miles, crossing the river on a cement bridge. Just past the bridge are two roads: one to the left leading to the White Chuck Campground, and a short one to the right leading to the Beaver Lake trailhead (elevation 900 feet).

Trail 629 is a level fifty- to sixty-year-old bed of a logging railroad operation through lush forest, following the Sauk River. The leafless old alders in winter are wrapped in yellow-green moss, which gives off an eerie glow on a gray day. Some of the trail has swampy areas or old sections of boardwalk, which children may enjoy stamping on. Many trees have pockets of licorice fern growing high out of their trunks, as in a tropical rain forest. In summer expect three-foot nettles alongside the trail; warn the kids not to touch them.

At 1½ miles the beaver engineers dammed streams flowing into the river in several places to form pools and islands. The sight of all these places to explore is exciting to little kids. Show them how to stop and listen for the warning slap of beaver tail on the water. Watch for signs: a ripple in the water, footprints in the mud, gnawed fallen saplings or stumps, the freshly built mound of a newly occupied beaver lodge. Continue on to find a split-log raised walkway and bridge over another, smaller lake with islands. In summer and fall, when the river is low, there are wading pools and picnic spots along the way.

10. Monte Cristo Railroad

Type: Dayhike
Difficulty: Moderate for children
Hikable: March–November
One way: 1¾ miles
High point: 1060 feet
Elevation gain: 200 feet
Green Trails map: No. 109 Granite Falls

This short trail, framed by moss-covered trees leaning over a spectacular river gorge, will appeal to all lovers of beauty, history, and adventure, and will fill any child with delight and wonder. It follows the railroad bed of the ore train that ran from Monte Cristo to Everett a hundred years ago. Washouts and slides have changed the surface, but occasional reminders of the train route remain. Although the trail is relatively easy, in a few places above the river slides have narrowed the railroad bed to only inches. Children should be watched carefully.

Drive I-5 to Everett, where you head east on U.S. Highway 2. Cross the Snohomish River and turn north onto State Highway 92 on the other side of the river. Drive to the center of Granite Falls and continue on the same road as it becomes the Mountain Loop Highway. Go 7.3 miles to a wooden sign on the right that reads "Old Robe Valley" opposite Forest Service Road No. 41. There is no parking lot, but the road shoulders are wide on both sides of the highway (elevation 1050 feet). This is private land: walk carefully and do not litter.

In the first half mile, drop 200 feet through forest and find a junction with two roads and a sign pointing toward the tunnels. Follow the trail right around a clear-cut toward the South Fork of the Stillaguamish River. (The river grows louder as you approach.) In April expect to find skunk cabbage, yellow violets, and papyruslike reeds in swampy places. Reach the river at ¾ mile, where you will find bigleaf maples with their elbows wrapped in moss, and an enormous, spreading old-growth Sitka spruce.

Because it is an old railroad grade, the trail is mostly level, but it does have several creeks to cross, a rock slide to scramble over, and that narrow section where a slip could be serious. The river gorge has wonderful white-water rapids and narrow channels enclosed by basalt cliffs.

When the railroad was being planned by the Rockefeller-Colby-Hoyt interests in 1892, a local engineer named M. Q. Barlow surveyed a route alongside the mountains but some distance above the river, saying that this route would avoid the effects of winter and spring washouts common in the Northwest. "Nonsense," said the New York financiers. "We have the best engineers in the world. This river is a mere trout stream compared to some they have surveyed, and straight down the river gorge is where this railroad will be built." Construction was completed in 1893 at a cost of millions of dollars.

In the winter of 1896 and again in 1897, floods reached the roofs of the tunnels, sweeping away all the timbers and ties. The railroad was rebuilt, and it reopened in 1900, but successive winter avalanches damaged the tracks, and from 1903 to 1907 no ore was shipped. From 1913 to 1920, some ore was shipped from Monte Cristo to Everett refineries, but by that time the Rockefeller financing had pulled out. Let's hope Barlow had the chance to say, "I told you so."

At 1 mile, duck the spray of a small waterfall on the right, and look for a remnant of old concrete and stone railroad grade. Occasional terracing and timber reinforcements show up from here on as the river descends into a canyonlike gorge. The first embedded railway ties appear about ¼ mile from the entrance to the gorge. Look to your left down a sheer drop of 50 feet to the raging Stillaguamish and to your right up a cliff wall. At 1⅓ miles you can see the dramatic entrance of Tunnel No. 6—a huge black hole blasted through the basalt, 300 feet long and nearly 30 feet high. Enter its jaws at 1⅔ miles. Children will be excited at the prospect of walking through it and listening to the sound of leaching water, but parents can be assured that the passage is clear and safe. You can use a flashlight to be sure of footing and to inspect the blasted ceiling and parts of old railroad

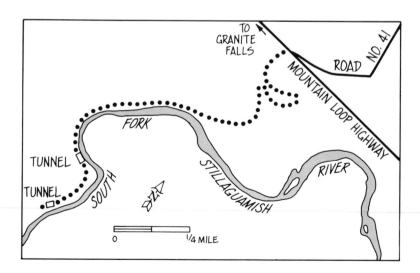

Entrance to Tunnel No. 5, Monte Cristo Railroad trail

ties, but you don't need one since there is light from the other end. It is a good turnaround point.

Beyond this tunnel the gorge narrows, and the river becomes wilder and noisier. In another ¼ mile find shorter tunnel, No. 5, only 100 feet long. Stop at the edge of the gorge for a snack and a view of the white-water rapids of the turbulent South Fork rushing by.

11. Thunder Creek

Type:	Dayhike or overnight
Difficulty:	Easy for children
Hikable:	June–November
One way to bridge:	1 mile
One way to campsites:	2 miles, 3.5 miles
High point:	1200 feet
Elevation gain:	None
Green Trails map:	No. 48 Diablo Dam
National Park Service map:	North Cascades National Park handout Backcountry permit required for camping

Thunder Creek drains water from many glaciers; their glacial silt colors Diablo Lake a startling turquoise green. Before starting this hike, families can gaze upward to the source: the glaciers on icy Colonial and Pyramid peaks. The trail along Thunder Creek's banks is nearly level and provides families a chance to walk among giant old-growth fir, western red cedar, and hemlock. Between the trunks and the creek are views of the bases of surrounding peaks many thousands of feet above. During the summer months, daily ranger-led nature walks provide children with information about the geology and botany of the North Cascades.

Drive the North Cascades Highway 20 east to Diablo Dam, and continue 4 miles beyond to Colonial Creek Campground. Turn into the

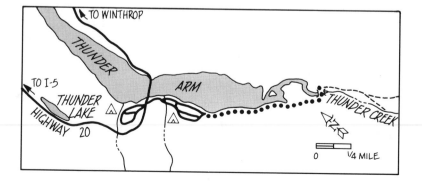

Giant cedar along Thunder Creek trail

right-hand campground. Backpackers must park just inside the entrance, but dayhikers can drive another 0.3 mile to the trailhead, located alongside the amphitheater (elevation 1200 feet).

The trail ambles along the scenic western shore of blue-green Thunder Arm of Diablo Lake. Little children and grandparents can feel great satisfaction on this lakeside section by walking only as far as the bench in the grove of 500-year-old western red cedars at ³/₄ mile. Here Thunder Arm merges into the multiple streambeds of Thunder Creek. But most children will want to hike at least as far as the suspension bridge at 1 mile. Kids enjoy the swaying possibilities of a suspension bridge and want to make it bounce.

Across the bridge the trail winds through the big trees to campsites at 2 and 3½ miles. The density of the North Cascades undergrowth tells the story of the annual rainfall here. Ask children to imagine what the first miners and explorers encountered without a trail. Occasionally the vine maples, ferns, devil's club, and salmonberries under the trees give way to glorious views of three mountains: ice-covered Snowfield, Tricouni (named for a kind of nailed boot once popular with climbers), and McAlister.

The trail continues for many more miles, gaining steadily, eventually entering the national park and providing climbers with access to surrounding high peaks. Families with children may content themselves with the 2½-mile campsite destination, because with it comes a sample of the beauty of the North Cascades.

12. Dam Traverse

Type:	Dayhike
Difficulty:	Difficult for children
Hikable:	June–November
One way to base of Ross Dam:	1³/₄ miles
One way to Lake Diablo:	5³/₄ miles
Elevation loss:	700 feet to the base of Ross Dam
Elevation gain:	500 feet to Lake Diablo
Green Trails map:	No. 48 Diablo Dam
National Park Service map:	North Cascades National Park handout

Adventure-loving families will love the challenge of crossing two dams of the Skagit River: a 389-foot-high Diablo Dam to drive across, and 540-foot-high Ross Dam to walk across. The reward for the short, steep descent is a close-up look at a major hydroelectric project for Seattle City Light in the heart of the North Cascades. With the aid of two cars, you could continue by trail to the level of the beautiful turquoise green waters of Diablo Lake. Be warned: keep a good hold on children when walking across Ross Dam, where pipes attached to the railing tempt little people to step up and lean over the railing.

Drive the North Cascades Highway 20 past Newhalem, crossing the Skagit River at the upper end of Gorge Lake, and continue another 7 miles to the Diablo Dam turnoff. With two cars, turn left, drive across the dam (one of the highlights of the trip for my children) and go to the end of the road, leaving one car just outside the Diablo Lake Resort. Back on the highway, continue another 4 miles to the Ross Lake trailhead on the left side of the highway (elevation 2200 feet).

Find the trail in the upper half of the parking area and drop steeply, crossing Happy Creek and switchbacking within sight of a series of small waterfalls. Children enjoy descending parallel to the water.

At approximately 1 mile and after a loss of 400 feet, reach a service road. Go right, and marvel at mammoth Ross Dam. As you look up fjordlike Ross Lake, imagine yourself in Norway. Then turn and gaze down the massive concave face of the dam. Keep a close eye on children, who may be tempted to climb the pipes alongside the railing as you cross.

This controversial structure has an interesting history. J. D. Ross, first head of Seattle City Light, proposed and executed a series of dams on the Skagit at a time when there was no environmental movement to protest the plan. Today the dams probably would not have been built. Throughout the 1960s and 1970s the threat of raising Ross Dam above its current level angered both Canadians, who did not want the lake to extend any farther into Canada, and the awakening American environmental movement, which opposed the loss of wilderness river valleys. The issue was finally settled in 1984, and Ross Dam will never be raised. Enough is enough.

"Why is the water above the dam a different color than the water

Ross Dam from Happy Creek trail

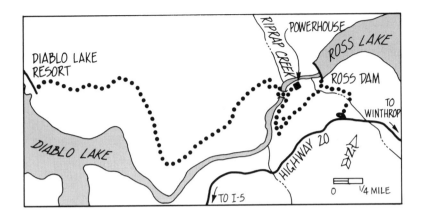

below?" my children asked. "Easy," answered their father. "They've taken all the electricity out of it." Actually, the water below Diablo Dam is not more clear, but Diablo Lake appears different because some of its water comes from glaciers that contain scoured rock from Skagit gneiss and granite, which colors the water an unearthly turquoise green. For an explanation of glacical scouring and a sample of Skagit gneiss, stop at the Diablo Lake overlook halfway between Diablo Lake and the Ross Dam pullout.

To continue the traverse, retrace your steps back to the junction with the service road and go straight ahead, following the road as it switchbacks for 3/4 mile, dropping another 300 feet to the powerhouse with its mysterious humming sound (elevation 1310 feet). Children will ask what it is doing to remove the electricity from the water. If you are lucky, a guided boat tour may be there just as you arrive, which will help answer children's questions.

Cross the Skagit River on a suspension bridge, and look back up at the towering dam, then climb by trail, switchbacking up the opposite side to gain 500 feet in 3/4 mile. For the next mile traverse the steep canyon wall—another place to hold on to children—with dramatic views down to Diablo Lake and across to the glaciers on glorious Colonial Peak that help turn Diablo Lake its color. The trail turns away from the river, and the remaining 2 miles to the lower trailhead are in forest.

13. Rainy Lake

Type: Dayhike
Difficulty: Easy for children
Hikable: Late July–October
One way: 1 mile
High point: 4900 feet
Elevation gain: 70 feet
Green Trails map: No. 50 Washington Pass
U.S. Forest Service map: Okanogan National Forest

Though it does not go downhill both directions, this trail is the next best thing. The only paved trail in the North Cascades Recreation Area, it offers a fine way for wheelchair-bound sightseers, or parents with babies in strollers, to see an alpine cirque lake rimmed by rocky cliffs and snowfields. Children can expect to see a large waterfall on the south cliff above the lakeshore, and a glacier on the crest high above it. Families can picnic at the trail's end and imagine themselves miles from the highway. The lake isn't suitable for swimming, so there isn't much for children to do when they get there, but the trail is so easy that they will enjoy the hike and have something to tell their friends about.

 Drive North Cascades Highway 20 east toward Winthrop. At Rainy Pass, turn west into the rest area and find the Rainy Lake trailhead

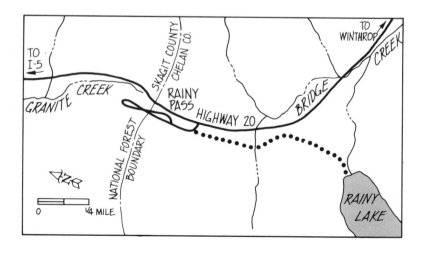

Rainy Lake after a snowstorm

on the highway's west side—on the same side road as the one leading
to the Lake Ann–Heather Pass Trail (elevation 4800 feet).

Dense, dark forest along the trail muffles the sound of cars by
$1/2$ mile. In fact, I found Audubon Society members at this point,
listening in deep forest for bird songs. Children can skip and run
ahead and back safely on the paved surface, but feel the wonder, hear
the sounds, and smell the smells of a North Cascade forest. The trail
ends at a viewing platform above the lake.

14. Cutthroat Lake

Type: Dayhike or overnight
Difficulty: Easy for children
Hikable: July–October
One way: 2 miles
High point: 4935 feet
Elevation gain: 400 feet
Green Trails map: No. 50 Washington Pass
U.S. Forest Service map: Okanogan National Forest

A shallow mountain lake beneath the towering cliffs of Cutthroat Peak is only 2 miles and one gentle showerbath waterfall from the highway. This is a great place for little children to wade and swim, while parents cast for the lake's namesake cutthroat trout in the clear waters. Boulders, grass, and reeds ring the lake. Families can camp ¼ mile from the shoreline, where there is a creek to play in and clumps of trees to hide in.

Drive North Cascades Highway 20 4.6 miles east of Washington Pass. Near the Cutthroat Creek bridge, turn uphill on Cutthroat Creek Road and go 1 mile to a trailhead parking lot (elevation 4580 feet). The trail's builders cut a wide swath through the trees for the benefit of horse riders, leaving very little shade on a hot day, so it's best to make this hike early or late in the day.

Find the trail at the west end of the parking area. Cross the bridge to the north side of Cutthroat Creek, and begin to climb gradually through pines and firs. At ⅓ mile look back at impressive Silver Star Mountain. Just before the lake, cross the creek again, then come to the first camping area, and a very rough trail that circles the lake. Cutthroat fishermen who want a higher vantage for casting may choose

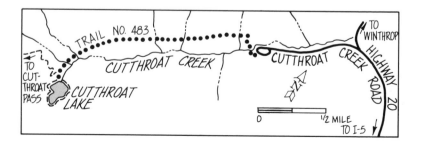

Wading in shallow Cutthroat Lake

the boulders at the north end of the lake. Older children like to jump into the water from them, which the fishermen may not appreciate.

I saw my first pine marten in trees near the lake here. He darted across the trail in front of me so fast I couldn't see him clearly, then climbed a tree close by and growled angrily from above my head at my invasion of his property.

Tiffany Lake

15. Tiffany Lake

Type:	Dayhike or overnight
Difficulty:	Easy for children
Hikable:	July–October
One way:	1 mile
High point:	6700 feet
Elevation gain:	200 feet on return
Green Trails map:	No. 53 Tiffany Mountain
U.S. Forest Service map:	Okanogan National Forest

This downhill hike for a short mile leads to a round, sparkling alpine lake with many campsites. On a hot summer day the chance to swim, wade, or fish can be especially inviting in the dry Okanogan.

The access road is long and can be rough on the family car, so it may be wise to check road conditions with the Winthrop ranger station before starting out.

Go east on North Cascades Highway 20 to the center of Winthrop. Find the East Chewach River Road and drive east 7.5 miles, passing the side road to Pearrygin Lake State Park. Just before the Chewach River bridge, go right on Forest Road No. 37. The road follows the river a short way, then heads back up. At 12.5 miles from the East Chewach River Road, go left on Forest Road No. 39. From here the road becomes rougher as it climbs Freezout Ridge, then drops again. At 7.5 miles from the 37–39 road junction, reach Tiffany Spring Campground and the trailhead (elevation 6700 feet).

The trail is smooth and downhill: children can easily skip down the whole way in a few minutes. It descends through old alpine fir forest bordered by Indian paintbrush, lupine, asters, golden stonecrop, and arnica to the lakeshore (elevation 6500 feet). Large campsites are located along the trail and near the outlet. The lake has logs and beaches for children to play on and swim from. Look straight up 1500 feet to imposing Tiffany Mountain standing guard above the lake.

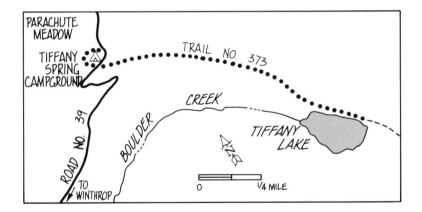

16. Domke Lake

Type:	Dayhike or overnight
Difficulty:	Difficult for children
Hikable:	July–October
One way:	3¼ miles
High point:	2200 feet
Elevation gain:	1100 feet
Green Trails map:	No. 114 Lucerne
U.S. Forest Service map:	Wenatchee National Forest

This warm forest lake set in an old glacier trough above Lake Chelan offers a unique mountain experience. Removed from the roar of powerboats, it is the site of a small, quiet resort. After traveling up chilly Lake Chelan, children will be happy to discover that Domke's water is warm enough for swimming and wading. The trail is short enough for a dayhike, but Domke Lake has enough attractions to justify staying overnight. When making plans, remember that rattlesnakes are sometimes found.

Drive to the town of Chelan, or go north on the east side of the lake outside the town on Lakeshore Road to Fields Point on Lake Chelan, and take the boat *Lady of the Lake* to Lucerne (elevation 1096 feet). In summer months the boat makes two round trips a day,

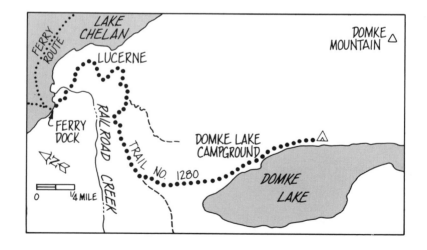

Lake Chelan from Domke Lake Trail

but this is subject to change, so check ahead. Plan to camp at Lucerne or at Domke Lake. From May 15 to September 10, the passenger boat leaves Chelan at 8:30 A.M., with a stop at Fields Point.

At Lucerne walk along the road for several hundred feet, cross Railroad Creek, and within ¼ mile find the Domke Lake Trail No. 1280. Throughout the first 250 feet of elevation gain, children can look down the lake they just cruised upon; the view is spectacular. Children will see water-skiiers, floatplanes, sailboats, and, beyond them, fruit orchards, then gradually hike above them all. The trail ascends through pine forest 1¹/₂ miles to another viewpoint. At 2½ miles the trail splits: the right fork goes to Emerald Park; you go left and in ¾ mile more come to large Domke Lake (elevation 2200 feet).

The concessionaire at the resort rents cabins and rowboats, and sells cold drinks. Swimming and fishing have been popular here for generations. If you wish to camp, you can continue along the trail to a U.S. Forest Service campground. Although there is no trail to the far side of the lake, if true privacy is your pleasure you can rent a boat and row to the campsites there. The kids will love the adventure.

17. Chelan Lakeshore

Type:	Dayhike or overnight
Difficulty:	Moderate for children
Hikable:	May–November
One way to Flick Creek:	4¹/₄ miles
High point:	1200 feet
Elevation gain and loss:	200 feet
Green Trails map:	No. 82 Stehekin
National Park Service map:	North Cascades National Park handout Backcountry permits required for camping

This shoreline trail alternately dips to water level, then rises to mount a rocky outcrop. Children will love hearing the sounds of lapping waves and small craft, and watching floatplanes landing and taking off. Some of the best beaches the trail passes are on private property, so do not assume they are all open to the public. Unfortunately, snakes are also found along this trail, and parents should be watchful. Rangers assured me that no one has ever reported a snake bite, but the snake I met got my respect, deference, and a wide detour. Early in the season they are less likely to be out, and early in the morning cool they are less likely to be active. If your kids are scared let them carry pebbles for throwing into shadows and bushes along the trail to check for snakes. If the family meets one, ask your kids afterward if they know what Emily Dickinson meant when after meeting a snake she said she felt "zero at the bone."

Flick Creek Campground and Four Mile Camp along the shoreline both have good campsites for several families.

Following the directions for Domke Lake (Hike 16), board the *Lady of the Lake*, but take it to the northern end of the lake, to

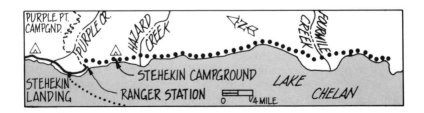

Stehekin Landing. The trail is clearly marked on the right side of the landing, just beyond the Golden West Information Center (elevation 1200 feet).

Begin your almost level stroll through ponderosa pine and dogwood forest. Pass alongside an enormous overhanging mossy rock and reach Hazard Creek at 1 mile. No hazards are apparent, but this makes a good turnaround point. Your children may be eager to stop and explore the creek as it enters the lake.

Continue through forest trail with occasional views out to Lake Chelan and its opposite south shore. Above Stehekin and the northwest end of the lake find the "Three B's"—Mount Buckner, Mount Booker, and Boston Peak. Another stream enters the lake at 4 miles—Fourmile Creek—and it makes an alternative campsite to Flick Creek, should that one be full. Children enjoy lakeshore camping and remember the fun of swimming in the cool waters long after leaving Lake Chelan.

Lake Chelan from Chelan Lakeshore trail

18. Stehekin River Trail

Type: Dayhike or overnight
Difficulty: Moderate for children
Hikable: June—October
One way: 3¹/₂ miles
High point: 1300 feet
Elevation gain: 100 feet
Green Trails map: No. 82 Stehekin
National Park Service map: North Cascades National
Park handout

Walk alongside a glacial river emptying into the head of Lake
Chelan. Your children can look for three beaver dams, cross seven
bridges, pass a small airfield with occasional landings and takeoffs,
and, in late September, watch for spawning coho salmon. Camp at
Weaver Point on the lake, then walk back to the bus pickup point
for the ride back down to Stehekin the next day.

To get to Stehekin, follow the directions for Chelan Lakeshore
(Hike 17). If you wish, bring your own bicycle to Stehekin and ride
up the road to Harlequin Camp—mostly on pavement. Otherwise,
catch the regularly scheduled bus out of town, and get off the shuttle
at Harlequin Camp (elevation 1200 feet), named for the unusual black-
and-white ducks that nest here. (You'll be lucky to see one.) The
driver may take you across the Stehekin River to the camp, or he or
she may leave you beside the bridge with a schedule and a warning
to be on time for your pickup.

Start on an old roadbed that passes through the camp and follow
it, passing a gate, after which it becomes trail. At the first footbridge
over a swamp, look right to find a meadow full of small seaplanes.
In an emergency Stehekin guests and residents can get to Chelan in
an hour. Children will want to see the planes taxi down the lake

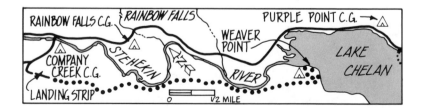

End of Stehekin River trail at Weaver Point Campground

before taking off, but you may not be able to catch sight of one while you are there. Continue walking through huge old-growth firs and ponderosa pines toward the river again on an almost-level trail. When you get to a wide, still pool lined with ferns and wild ginger, tell the children it isn't just a pool—it's a beaver pond, created by a dam your children can see. This is the first of a series of dams built by the forest's aquatic architects. Alongside at least one dam, I saw teeth

Logging operation across Stehekin River trail

marks in the trunks of trees, indicating a new resident had returned to the site of the old colony. Several beaver-cut trees lay across the trail.

The first view of the river after leaving Harlequin Camp comes at 1½ miles. Look for a big bend in the channel around a gravel bar, with a grassy open slope across the river—perhaps an old homestead pasture—then drop to the level of the swift-flowing water. Tell the kids the silt comes from twelve glaciers on surrounding peaks, and is particularly noticeable after a rain. Huge old cedars lean out over rock bars. Climb up steeply and away from the river again and walk through more forest. If the children are whiny, promise that they will cross more bridges and drop down to the river again to a sandy bar at low water from which they can wade and paddle. After September rains, mushrooms begin erupting out of the forest floor. It is never safe for kids to taste them, but the wild raspberries along the trail are safe and delicious.

Occasionally a big tree will have a huge tangle of tight extra growth containing dead twigs and branches. Tell the kids this is the result of a tree virus called witches' broom. In the semigloom alongside enormous moss-covered rock walls, it is fun for kids to imagine the witch herself. Would she look like the Wicked Witch of the West, riding the broom across the sky and cackling, "Just you wait, my pretty one"?

Cross a rocky flood plain of DeVore Creek at 3.3 miles, washed out by a flash flood in the spring of 1948. Take the hikers' bridge and find yourself at Weaver Point Campground. Boaters take some of the waterfront sites, but they also get the uplake wind there. Choose a more protected spot in the trees and have the children look for an old homestead apple tree planted by settlers decades ago and still bearing sweet apples, tempting to deer. In late September you can also look for returning coho salmon, planted at the mouth of the Stehekin, that have gone down to Chelan and are returning to spawn. (They spend their lives in the lake.) A fisherman passed me on the trail with one he claimed weighed five pounds.

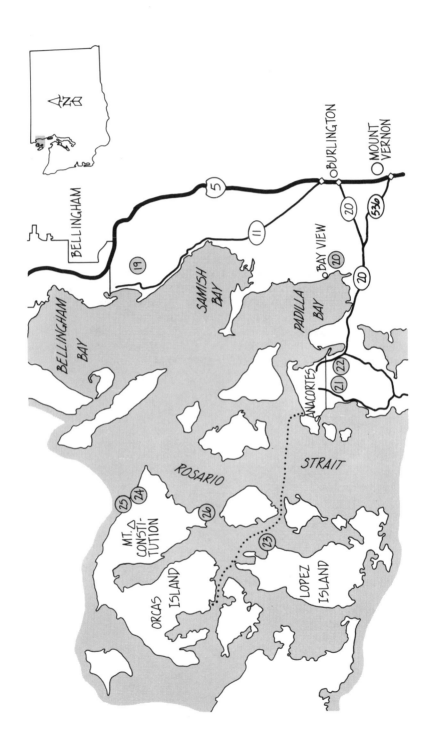

Bellingham, Anacortes, and the San Juans

19. Fragrance Lake

Type: Dayhike
Difficulty: Moderate for children
Hikable: Year-round
One way: 2 miles from trailhead, and
¼ mile from access road
High point: 1030 feet
Elevation gain: 900 feet
Map: Larrabee State Park brochure

This beautiful 2-mile trail through low-elevation old-growth cedars and firs leads upward to a serene woodland lake. It can also be reached by a ¼-mile short version trail if your time is short or your children are very young. However, the long way has the most to offer and is recommended for older children. The long way also has a view of boats in Wildcat Bay. Downed nurse logs supporting young hemlocks are common, but children will laugh at the sight of a nurse rock at about 1 mile, with tree roots wrapping the oblong rock like cord around a

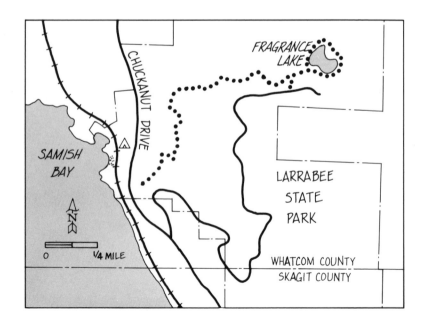

Fragrance Lake

package. Fragrance Lake is crescent-shaped, has trout and skipping water bugs, and can be circled on a level shoreline trail. Ask your children how they think this lake got its name.

Drive I-5 north of Mount Vernon to Exit 231 and go west and north 15 miles on Chuckanut Drive (Highway 11) to Larrabee State Park. (From Bellingham go south on Chuckanut Drive to the park.) To the north, across from the two entrance roads is a parking place for four or five cars, a trail sign, and the trailhead (elevation 130 feet). For the shorter route, go south of the entrance 0.2 mile, turn uphill, and drive 2.2 miles, to within 0.25 mile of the lake.

From the first trailhead, begin upward. In about 150 yards cross what is left of the old Interurban Railway right of way and continue upward, gaining elevation in steep switchbacks. Fire apparently swept up the hillside five or ten years ago, because the bases of a number of massive firs are recently blackened. The trail is in fine condition and even provides a bench at one point where families can pause to listen to birds. We watched a nuthatch rhythmically bobbing up and down, and inspected pileated woodpecker holes as rectangular as window frames. In about 1 mile make a short side trip left to face the view over Samish Bay. Children can gaze out to Fidalgo, Cypress, Orcas, Samish, and Lummi islands, then laugh as they look straight down on the boats and rafts bobbing in Wildcat Cove beneath them. Return to the sometimes muddy trail, drop down to cross a small creek on a bridge, and continue left and upward.

Intercept the shorter trail ¼ mile before the lake. Mountain bikers have discovered the lake-circling trail, and a number of them join

hikers on the trail here. Be prepared for the possibility that one will come upon you suddenly. Not all riders are as cautious as they should be, and short kids may be hidden by the brush until the last second.

Your first view of the lake is screened by tall salmonberry bushes, alders, and maples. Not to worry, as the shoreline is clearly accessible a bit farther along. A Tinkertoy-shaped maple with right-angled bends in its trunk bears investigation by families with small children here.

The lake surface (elevation 1030 feet) is smooth, and on a clear day reflects Chuckanut Mountain. The morning we were there a pair of American widgeons skidded to a landing across the water.

20. Padilla Bay Natural Estuarine Research Reserve and Shore Trail

Type: Dayhike
Difficulty: Easy for children
Hikable: Year-round
One way: 2¼ miles
High point: 10 feet
Elevation gain: None
Map: Available from Breazeale Interpretive Center

Looking west across the bay to the Swinomish Slough bridge, children can see the Cherry Point oil refineries, Fidalgo Island, and Mount Erie. At any time of year this trail along Padilla Bay holds a shoreline fascination for kids. An interpretive center helps to enrich their experience. In the reserve they will always see ducks and gulls; if they are lucky they may see raccoons, small rodents, and fish, along with distant oil tankers and pleasure craft.

The trail is a level, gravel-surfaced dike. One end begins alongside saltwater bay, and the other follows a mud-banked stream out to the bay. Advance arrangements can be made for handicapped or stroller access, and a handicap-designated parking area is located at the south end.

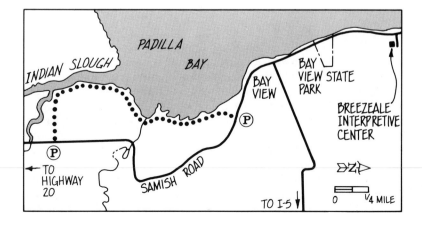

Beachcombing along the Padilla Bay shore

Visit the Breazeale Interpretive Center first for information about animals and birds to look for, and a "hands-on" room where children can touch and examine stuffed examples of these creatures. (Parents should go along to help.) You will also find there a good explanation of the effect of a freshwater estuary on a saltwater bay. Edna Breazeale donated her land for this nature reserve; the State Department of Ecology and the Skagit County Park System cooperated to preserve this dike trail and to build the interpretive center. The center is closed Monday and Tuesday.

 Drive I-5 north of Mount Vernon and take Exit 231. Briefly follow Chuckanut Drive (Highway 11), then make an immediate left on Wilson Road (which becomes Johnson Road), and drive west 7 miles to the community of Bay View. Turn right on the Bay View–Edison Road and go 1 mile, passing Bay View State Park to the interpretive center. After viewing the exhibits, go back the way you came, driving past Wilson Road, and go to Second Street. Parking for the trail is up the hill and on the left side of the street. With a young family, take two cars and leave one at each end. Parking at the far end of the trail is 2.2 miles farther along the road, next to a creek.

Squeeze through the narrow entrance gate to the raised dike trail that follows an S-curved bay. These dikes were built on the Skagit River after 1870 to push back the sea and to produce fertile farmland, but salt marsh wetland habitat for birds and animals was removed in the process. Since then, in some places, the salt marsh has returned, and now there is a slight chance children will see harbor seals, muskrats, and otters if the tide is in, and gulls, blue herons, eagles, and ducks among the old piling stumps if the tide is out. At the mouths of rivers such as the Skagit, where fresh and salt water mix, estuaries provide a home to a rich variety of plants and animals that can tolerate salt and are especially adapted to tidal marshes.

Look across Padilla Bay to oil refineries and the Skagit mud flats at ¼ mile. Imagine the impact of a major oil spill here. At ¾ mile, head around a curving cove into No Name Slough. Wind around Indian Slough at 1¼ miles, heading inland to the tidal marsh at 1¾ miles and the parking area at 2¼ miles. When the tide is down, have children look for eelgrass, its roots planted in thick mud, and for mud snails, found in great numbers on the mud flats and relished as food by many animals. (No, this would not be a good place to play, tempting as the mud may be to kids.) Halfway along the bay, the trail heads inland among fields of crops. We saw migrant workers picking baby cucumbers for pickles when we walked the trail in the fall. Follow the muddy streambed inland to the trail's end at 2¼ miles, where schools of tiny baby salmon may sometimes be seen to be swimming out to sea. There are sure to be ducks and geese in the marsh here and remnants of pilings of the old piers from long ago.

21. Sugarloaf Mountain

Type:	Dayhike
Difficulty:	Moderate for children
Hikable:	Year-round
One way:	1 mile
High point:	1055 feet
Elevation gain:	200 feet
Map:	Anacortes Community Park Lands

Kids can climb a small mountain and see a magnificent panorama of the San Juan Islands, the Olympic Mountains, Lake Erie, Whidbey Island, and the Strait of Juan de Fuca as the reward for this short summit hike. The views are almost as good as those from Mount Erie, but your children will not be crowded by motorbikes and the mobs who drive to the summit on a clear day. Take a lunch and a map, and plan to watch ship traffic in the strait, the sailboats on Lake Erie,

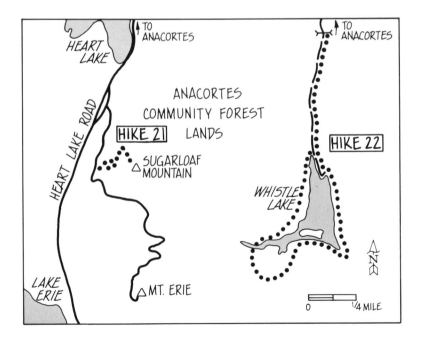

Sugarloaf Mountain and Lake Erie

and to soak in the beauty of the drowned mountain range that has become the San Juans.

Drive I-5 north to the Burlington exit and take North Cascades Highway 20 west towards Anacortes. Where Highway 20 divides, turn left on a road signed "DECEPTION PASS." In 2 miles the road divides again between Lake Campbell Road and an unsigned road leading toward Mount Erie. Take this road right for 1.5 miles.

At the next junction take a right up Auld Drive to Mount Erie. Go 0.7 mile to the Sugarloaf Mountain trailhead and a small parking space, marked Trail No. 215 (elevation 750 feet).

Head upward on a narrow trail among rock outcrops covered with moss and lichen, and through woodland areas. Many alternative trails thread across the mountain, some switchbacking, others leading directly upward. Any will get you to the top, so choose the one whose grade best suits your children. Kids may find the network of possible routes confusing, and want to know which is the "real trail"? They are all real. Close to the summit, a dying tree dropped an arching limb just over the trail in the winter of 1989. Stepping under it, children may feel as if they are walking into a picture frame. In ⅓ mile, expect to find the first view westward toward Lake Erie and the strait.

A moss-covered rounded rock outcrop, which would be termed a "bald" in the Great Smokies, is Sugarloaf's summit. With a map, help children identify Skagit, Kiket, and Hope islands to the southeast, Mount Erie to the south, and the western shores of Whidbey Island. At any time of the year the views are glorious.

22. Whistle Lake

Type: Dayhike
Difficulty: Easy for children
Hikable: Year-round
One way: ³/₅ mile
High point: 430 feet
Elevation gain: None
Map: Anacortes Community Park Lands

This gorgeous former city watershed has become the Anacortes Community Forest Lands. Because it has been protected for decades, Whistle Lake and its network of forest trails and overlooks have a quiet woodland beauty. The wonder is that because of the low elevation, this area can be enjoyed at any time of year. Children will think that the lake, seen from several overlooks, is like a wilderness fjord, with its rocky cliffs, steep island, and forested shoreline. Teenagers have a great time leaping off the vertical cliffs. (Be sure to check depths before leaping anywhere.) With life vests younger children can safely play on the steep shore or swim in the deep lake. The day we were there a platoon of small, happy children were all swimming and splashing, wearing life vests.

Though it has been logged, the 2200-acre park still contains some old-growth firs, a flourishing grove of madronas, and many mature cedars and hemlocks. The 25 miles of numbered trails and old road-beds are designated for different kinds of use: some are for hiking only, and others are open to bicycles, motorcycles, and horses.

 Follow North Cascade Highway 20 west toward Anacortes, and stay right where it divides. Follow the highway spur to its end on Commercial Avenue in Anacortes. Instead of following the main route into the city, turn left and go 0.3 mile to Commercial Avenue's end. Go left again for 1 block, then turn right on Hillcrest, past a cemetery, and turn right again on Whistle Lake Road. Go 1.3 miles to the end of the pavement and a junction. Go left, following signs to Whistle Lake and a large parking lot, crowded on weekends, some 2 miles from Highway 20. Walk the gated road approximately ³/₅ mile to the lake. Most families stop here for the best swimming, but if you have the energy, follow the up-and-down 2½-mile trail that circles the lake. It has fascinating views of the island, Toot Swamp, and private picnic spots, but poor swimming for young children. No campfires are allowed.

Whistle Lake

Though the spiderweb of trails is complex, rewards in the Anacortes Community Forest Lands are great. We heard a varied thrush one March day, saw several of the best examples of standing old firs riddled with woodpecker-drilled holes, glimpsed the red flash of a pileated woodpecker's head, and felt the warmth of sunlight filtering through old forest canopy.

Note: A map of the Whistle Lake–Heart Lake area can be ordered for $2.50 plus postage from Anacortes Community Forest Lands (ACFL), P.O. Box 547, Anacortes, WA 98221.

23. Spencer Spit

Type:	Dayhike or overnight
Difficulty:	Easy for children
Hikable:	Year-round
One way:	$1/2$ mile
High point:	10 feet
Elevation gain:	None
Washington State Parks map:	Spencer Spit State Park

A child-fascinating sand spit encloses a saltwater lagoon in a state park on Lopez Island. Homesteaded at the beginning of the century, the spit houses a rebuilt replica of the original cabin at its tip, inviting children to come and play in it. Two mirages may disappoint them, however: no, the spit does not reach Frost Island (there is a deep swift channel separating them), and no, they cannot play in the lagoon and marsh. These are fragile areas reserved for birds and other marine life. But abundant other activities present themselves to kids, and they will not want to leave Spencer Spit.

From the ferry landing on Lopez Island, drive 1.1 miles on Ferry Road to the first road junction, turn left on Port Stanley Road. In 2.5 miles, turn left onto Baker View Road, continuing on to the park in another 0.5 mile. Drive to the picnic area–restrooms parking lot near the beach (elevation 50 feet).

Drop to the beach on a 100-yard-long wooded trail. Though the spit is shaped like a hollow triangle, because of outflow creeks, only one leg of the triangle can be walked to the spit's end. A half-mile-long built-up trail makes easy walking for small kids, but so does the gently sloping, south-facing beach. Digging for cockles, mussels, butter clams, horse clams, and geoducks is excellent during low tides. Water heated by the sun as it returns over tide flats is warm enough for children to swim in. Within the spit, in the marshy lagoon, kids can look for gulls, ducks, great blue herons, geese, and many sandpipers— large and small.

The old log cabin is a magnetic feature, drawing children in to explore and speculate about what it was like to live there. Did home-steaders live mainly on clams and fish? What was it like during winter storms? A picnic table inside invites families to come in, perhaps take shelter from the wind, and munch on sandwiches. Fires should be built only in the circular firepits provided.

A mandatory walk to the farthest point of the spit provides more

Children's playhouses made of driftwood on Spencer Spit

questions. Will the spit keep on growing? Will it ever reach Frost Island across the narrow stretch of water? Why not?

Walk-in campsites along the shoreline make it possible for families to camp and enjoy the beauty of the San Juans, lighted ferryboats coming and going, and views of Mount Baker by sunset and sunrise.

Mountain Lake and Mount Constitution

24. Mountain Lake Loop

Type:	Dayhike or overnight
Difficulty:	Moderate for children
Hikable:	March–November
Loop trip:	4 miles
High point:	1200 feet
Elevation gain and loss:	400 feet
Washington State Parks map:	Moran State Park handout

What child could resist walking through forest on this wide, gentle trail, sometimes at lake level, sometimes 100 feet above it? Waves lap and slurp alongside. Fish jump and jump again. In April, May, and June, ospreys swoop and cry to hikers, almost as if taunting them. Take a lunch and find a sandy beach at the halfway point where the kids can splash and swim.

 From the Orcas Island ferry landing, follow signs to Moran State Park. Enter the park and drive to the Olga–Mount Constitution Road intersection. Turn left on Mount Constitution Road; 2 miles from the intersection turn right to Mountain Lake Landing. Park beside the old ranger cabins and dock (elevation 1100 feet).

Begin by hiking counterclockwise, following the shore to Cascade Creek, the lake's outlet creek, and a tiered concrete dam, built to supply water to the community of Olga. Drop below the dam, passing a trail to Cascade Creek, and briefly follow a construction road. Pass a trail for Mount Pickett, then bear left on the lake trail, skirting its shore. Old snags standing in the water have attracted woodpeckers and other birds. Children can listen for their rat-a-tat and the haunting sounds of ospreys' calls. The trail zigzags away from the lake through forest, then begins a gradual climb to high, mossy rock bluffs with the best views of Mount Constitution on a clear day. Kids will enjoy switchbacking steeply down through mossy rocks to the lake level again. They may wonder about the rocky islands stretched along the length of the lake. Have these islets been explored? Could they walk out on a tiny peninsula and swim to the closest one?

In shallow coves at the north end of the lake, kids can wade and swim in the cool water. In 2¾ miles from the trailhead, find a branching trail leading to Twin Lakes (Hike 25). Keep left through an open glade of alders and maples and round the lake's end. Much salvage logging has been done here, necessitated by the windfalls of the winter of 1990. Shady groves still exist alongside inlets and bays on the west side of Mountain Lake, however, sheltering a few areas shallow enough for kids to swim in. The east side has at least two 100-foot climbs, plus numerous ups and downs. The west side has one high point. Continue to the trail's starting point and a walk-in camping area on a little peninsula.

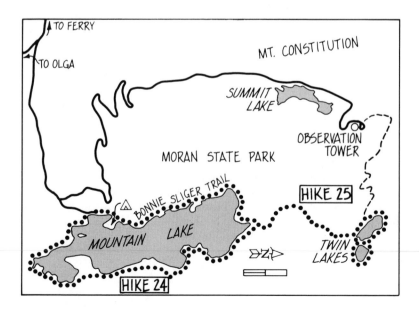

25. Twin Lakes

Type:	Dayhike or overnight
Difficulty:	Moderate for children
Hikable:	March–November
One way:	2¹⁄₈ miles
High point:	1300 feet
Elevation gain:	200 feet
Washington State Parks map:	Moran State Park handout

These two enchanting little lakes on a ridge below Mount Constitution will appeal to children, who will find them just their size. Fishing is good in both of them, and though the water is cold, swimming is possible in their shallow coves. A good campsite on the southeast shore of the smaller lake would make a private family camp for one family.

 Follow the directions to Mountain Lake Landing (Hike 24).

Begin hiking clockwise on the Bonnie Sliger Trail from the parking area beside the campground on Mountain Lake. The trails here were originally built by the Civilian Conservation Corps in the 1930s, but this one was improved and named for a young Youth Conservation Corps supervisor who died from a fall at nearby Doe Bay in 1977. Children love walking alongside the deep blue-green larger Mountain Lake, with its coves and rocky islands sheltered by old trees. At 1¹⁄₄ miles, leave the loop trail at a junction and follow a brook uphill for ¹⁄₂ mile. The trail levels off and passes startling reed-filled ponds in the midst of deep forest, preparing kids for the lakes before they see them. A brushy trail circles the larger twin in ³⁄₅ mile. Only a small ridge of 50 yards separates it from the second twin. The smaller lake has lily pads and water skippers, and may remind kids of a garden fishpond, but as they follow its ²⁄₅ mile trail, the sheltering old trees, the mossy rocks on the lake's north side, and the sound of the outfall creek tumbling north to Rosario Strait will bring them back to the reality of the mountain-on-an-island setting. Kids particularly enjoy the trail circling the smaller lake because it has a rocky, mossy outcrop to climb on and a reedy swamp with bridges to stomp across. Complete the circuit by passing a fork for Mount Pickett, then return to the trail leading back along the west side of Mountain Lake to the trailhead.

First Twin Lake and Mount Constitution

26. Obstruction Pass

Type:	Dayhike or overnight
Difficulty:	Easy for children
Hikable:	Year-round
One way to beach:	$1/2$ mile
High point:	100 feet
Elevation loss:	100 feet
Map:	San Juan County road map

A secluded Orcas Island beach offers children good beachcombing, with small coves on the west side that are safe for wading and swimming. Reach this Department of Natural Resources (DNR) Recreation Area and Campsite by a short forest walk to a pebble beach. Kids can watch for kayakers, who like to put in on this beach.

From the ferry landing, follow signs to Olga, going northeast around East Sound. One-quarter mile before the town, turn east on a road signed to Doe Bay. In another 0.5 mile turn south on the Obstruction Pass Road, which winds around an open valley, then heads south. One mile from the Doe Bay intersection, a gravel road to the right is signed to Obstruction Pass with the DNR logo. Follow this road for 1 mile to the trailhead (elevation 100 feet).

Begin hiking on a level trail through mixed alder and fir forest with much windfall from the great Siberian Express storm of 1989 and two northeasterlies of 1990. Lush ferns and salal enrich the trail above East Sound, but steep banks and drop-offs near the end of the trail

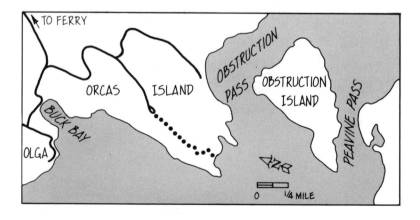

End of Obstruction Pass trail

mean children should not run ahead or be unaccompanied. Short side
trails lead to cliffs above the water that offer views up East Sound
to Olga and Rosario Resort. At ½ mile the trail reaches a walk-in
campground, circles the camp area, then drops 15 feet to the crescent-shaped beach and views of the west side of Orcas and Lopez
islands, with ferries approaching and leaving Upright Head on Lopez.

At high tide children will enjoy playing on the steep pebbled
beach, especially looking for agates and other treasures. At low tide
they can explore tide pools on either side of the bay. Kayakers wearing
hooded wet suits frequently arrive or depart, providing entertainment
for curious children, and yachts sometimes sail in to tie to one of the
mooring buoys just offshore. Other views from this beach are of
Obstruction and Blakely islands; if you look to the east, Frost Island
off Spencer Spit (Hike 23) may be seen.

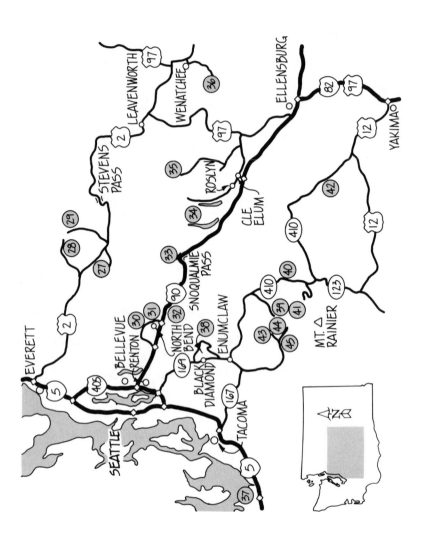

Stevens Pass to Mount Rainier

27. Lake Elizabeth

Type:	Dayhike or overnight
Difficulty:	Easy for children
Hikable:	March–November
Loop trip:	1 mile
High point:	2900 feet
Elevation gain:	None
Green Trails map:	No. 174 Mt. Si
U.S. Forest Service map:	Mt. Baker–Snoqualmie

Kids love this lake. It is a fine weekend destination for family recreation: camping, fishing, swimming, and exploring. As evidence, four happy kids under six came up to me with their frog collection as soon as I got out of the car. Later, as I walked around the lake, I heard them swimming and calling, "I'm up to my belly button, Mom!" You can drive your family here if your car can handle the rough, rocky road. The short hike around the lake provides a choice of opportunities for camping, fishing, and swimming. Hiking makes an excellent way of warming up after a swim in Elizabeth's cold waters.

 Drive east on U.S. Highway 2; between mileposts 45 and 46, turn right at the signed Money Creek Campground. Cross the river and drive 1 mile on the Old Cascade Highway, turn right (south) onto the Miller River Road No. 6410 for 0.1 mile, then turn right again onto Money Creek Road No. 6420 and drive 7 miles to Lake Elizabeth

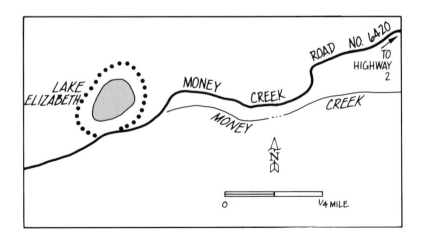

Lake Elizabeth

(elevation 2900 feet). This is a sometimes road, sometimes passable and sometimes not. Check with the Skykomish Ranger District—(206) 677-2414—before leaving home.

Begin on level Trail No. 1071, lined with skunk cabbage, Labrador tea, and some wonderful old-growth Alaska cedars. There are at least three possible campsites along the way. Logs along the shoreline provide casting points for fishermen or jumping-off points for swimmers and waders. We even watched a raft being launched from one. The portion of the trail on the north side of the lake has a steep side slope, closing in with salmonberries and bracken, but the trail returns to the shade of old trees before you come back to the starting point. This trail gets little maintenance, so expect to cross over logs and fight brush. The scenery around the lake is spectacular. In the early summer multiple waterfalls pour from cliffs high above the road.

28. Troublesome Creek

Type: Dayhike
Difficulty: Easy for children
Hikable: March–November
Loop trip: ¹/₂ mile
High point: 1258 feet
Elevation gain: 25 feet
Green Trails map: No. 143 Monte Cristo
U.S. Forest Service map: Mt. Baker–Snoqualmie

This marvelous short, old-growth loop trail crosses Troublesome Creek twice within ¹/₂ mile. Though it is labeled a nature trail, there are no interpretive signs, but you will find plenty of benches at beauty spot viewpoints where parents of small children can pause, rest, and talk about the cycle of renewal in old-growth forest. There is such a magical feel to this place that your children will almost expect to see Hansel and Gretel tiptoeing through the forest ahead of them.

Drive east on U.S. Highway 2 toward Stevens Pass. Turn left at the Index turnoff onto County Road No. 63, and travel 1 mile to a bridge. Instead of going into Index, stay on County Road No. 63 for 10.3 miles to Troublesome Creek Campground. Drive through the

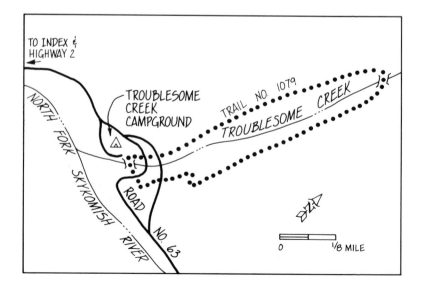

Troublesome Creek trail bridge

campground to the lower level and find the trailhead (elevation 1258 feet).

Start your hike on either side of the creek; the loop is good either way. It is described here going counterclockwise. Begin by passing the lower footbridge, and starting upstream alongside it. If you begin on the right side, you will travel past enormous old cedars and firs. Some of the cedars have been dying back for centuries; circling their girth would require eight to ten children. Ask your children to guess how old the trees might be. Look for young and middle-aged trees interspersed with the ancient ones. The first miners to come to the Skykomish River valley used this creek to get to gold, silver, and copper claims high above. At the farthest point upstream, the constructed trail ends next to a 500-year-old fir tree and a bench. Just around the other side of the fir is a large flat rock beside the creek, suitable for a picnic spread. Stop to rest and enjoy the tumbling creek and its unusual colors, caused by dissolved minerals in the water.

Turn and start downstream again, crossing the creek on the upper footbridge. Old, unmaintained side trails (perhaps remnants of miners' trails) depart from the main trail in several places, calling to children to explore them as far as they go, but some of the old trails dead-end near the water and may not be safe for exploring. Hiking alongside the creek is never troublesome, despite the name. The stream has a spellbinding beauty, particularly when its rapids break over water-scoured bedrock. Along the bank in summer low-water times are small rocky beaches where children might safely play. Mossy skeletons of old trees frame outlooks over white-water rapids. Pass under a rock bridge, cross over the first footbridge again, and return to your car, feeling a bit as if you are returning from Alice's Wonderland up through the rabbit hole.

29. Evergreen Mountain

Type: Dayhike
Difficulty: Difficult for children
Hikable: July–October
One way: 1¹/₂ miles
High point: 5587 feet
Elevation gain: 1300 feet
Green Trail map: No. 143 Monte Cristo
U.S. Forest Service map: Mount Baker–Snoqualmie

(Note: In 1992, the last 3 miles of road were closed; contact the Forest Service for current information.)

A spectacular 360-degree viewpoint and a former lookout and aircraft-spotting station lie at the top of this short, steep trail. Driving the access road is like driving part of the trail. Older children will love climbing to the top of the mountain and surveying the meadows, ridges, and forests below, as did former lookouts. Luscious blueberries ripen in August and September. Carry water as there is none on the trail and none at the lookout.

Drive east on U.S. Highway 2 and turn left onto the Index Road. Travel past the town of Index upriver on the North Fork Skykomish River Road No. 63 to the junction with Road No. 65 at 14.5 miles. You will pass Troublesome Creek and San Juan campgrounds, both good

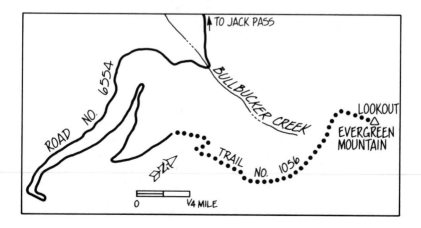

Evergreen Mountain trail

base camps for hiking this trail. Turn right and follow Road No. 65 for 2.5 miles steeply up to Jack Pass. (If you are traveling west from the east side of the Cascades on U.S. Highway 2, turn before Skykomish onto the Beckler River Road No. 65, and stay on it all the way to Jack Pass, approximately 13 miles.) Once at Jack Pass by either road, turn left onto Road No. 6550 and head down-valley for approximately 1 mile to a fork and turn left again onto Road No. 6554. Drive cautiously: the road becomes steep and narrow, and has washout areas for the next 8 miles. Make a right turn onto Road No. 6554-610 and go another mile to Trail No. 1056 (elevation 4300 feet).

Get out of the car and marvel at views in every direction. Look north to the spectacular Monte Cristo peaks, and Bears Breast, Cathedral, and Daniel. Listen for the sounds of bees in the alpine flowers, and for bird songs. (The one who seems to be calling "Quick, three beers" is the olive-sided flycatcher.) Children should know that Evergreen Mountain burned out of control for most of the summer of 1967, and that no one expected it ever to be green again. Yet today, looking up through snags and stumps, the remnants of that fire, you will find green meadows and twenty-three-year-old alpine and noble firs. The mountain is renewing itself.

Start uphill steeply through the clear-cut of fire-damaged timber from the old burn. The meadow flowers are amazingly diverse and continuously in bloom. We saw masses of blazing golden arnica, glacier lilies, penstemon, lupine, columbine, tiger lilies, and paintbrush amid clumps of little trees. At ¼ mile the trail surmounts a ridge and gives views south to Mount Rainier and peaks beyond. Stop here and enjoy the sounds of sighing winds and sights of alpine serenity. At ½ mile reach a stand of old trees that escaped the flames and provides shade today. The steepness of the trail eases a bit before coming out of the trees into a little saddle (elevation 5300 feet). If your family does not wish to get to the lookout, this makes a good turnaround point.

Traveling up from the saddle in midsummer is a treat for any family because of the exceptional show of brightly colored wildflowers. Continue another ⅓ mile up the steep east side of the mountain to the closed lookout, built in 1935. Sit down and bring out the lemonade. Tell children that this fire lookout was used during the war as an aircraft-spotting station. Bring a good Forest Service map to help you identify the many peaks, rivers, and valleys from the 360-degree span. The sensation of having climbed to the top of a mountain on a clear day is one children will cherish forever.

30. Snoqualmie Falls

Type: Dayhike
Difficulty: Easy for children
Hikable: Year-round
One way: ¹/₂ mile
High point: 120 feet
Elevation gain: Minimal
Map: None

A short hike to the base of a 268-foot waterfall, so beautiful the Indians considered it a sacred place, is easy at any time of year. Puget Power has harnessed its force and provided the combination of road and trail, but the rocky riverbed beach, sandbars, bedrock benches, caves, and pools have been appropriated by kids and families. On one hot summer day, believe it or not, we saw fishermen trying their luck in the pool directly below the falls. Parents were carrying tiny babies in backpacks, a nine-year-old told me he had made it to the other side of the river by swimming across, and several six- to eight-year-olds were exploring water-carved caves directly below the observation platform 268 feet above. Despite the crowd, there was no sense of invasion of privacy because the roar of water drowned out all voices.

 Officially the trail starts near the Snoqualmie Falls Visitors Center and descends ¹/₂ mile to the powerhouse, but most people start at the lower parking lot as described here. Take I-90 to Exit 22 and drive

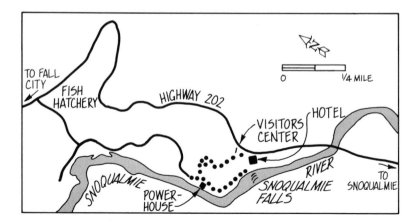

Snoqualmie Falls

to Fall City. From there go north on State Route 202, signed "NORTH
BEND." At 2.4 miles go right on 372nd Avenue S.E. and continue for
0.7 mile to the road's end (elevation 120 feet).

   Begin by walking around the power station gate and down a paved
road to the station house. Beside it, the bank serves as a launching
point for kayaks, canoes, and rafts. Children will want to gaze at the
interesting craft bobbing and balancing in the eddying current in

front of them. Pass the trail from the Visitors Center and take the second trail behind the power station. Part of this trail is completely enclosed with fencing, like a cage. Kids can look through powerhouse windows to the turbines generating power for 16,000 homes from the waterfall. On the other side of the cage, you can follow the trail either down to the rocky riverbed or on a fenced boardwalk to a dead-end viewpoint of the falls.

To continue beyond the viewpoint, walk back toward the powerhouse and find a short path to the river level. Once on the riverbed, proceed through boulders toward the waterfall as close as you wish. In midsummer when water levels are low, children stop to wade in pools at the river's edge. Families find niches and boulders along the bank for picnicking in the mist and spray. At the base of the majestic falls, people stop and stare wordlessly upward at the plunging, free-falling curtain of water. The sight is so compelling it is hard to turn away.

31. Little Si

Type: Dayhike
Difficulty: Difficult for children
Hikable: Year-round
One way: 5 miles
High point: 2000 feet
Elevation gain: 1500 feet
Map: None

Too many beginners with children take on the Mount Si Trail, which proves to be so difficult that the kids may never want to hike again. Overlooked is kid-size Little Si, also difficult but more realistic and offering children the challenge and satisfaction of climbing to a rocky summit with a view. Along the way is a wonderful mossy forest and an old rock slide to travel through before starting up. For years to come, children will see Mount Si from the freeway, look for the cliff separating the two Si's, and point with pride to the little mountain they have climbed.

Drive east on I-90 to North Bend and take Exit 31. Exactly 1.0 mile from the east edge of town turn left on 432nd S.E. and cross the bridge over the Middle Fork Snoqualmie River. Park beside the bridge. Turn left to walk ¼ mile east through homes to the signed trailhead, elevation 500 feet.

The trail starts up steeply at first, then forks several times. Turn

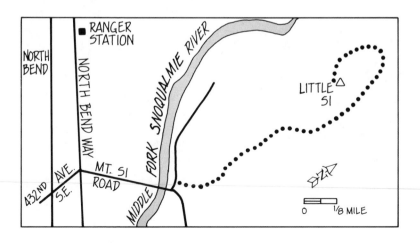

Top of Little Si under the towering west face of Mount Si

left consistently at each fork. Trails leading up or right go to Mount Si, but none of the forks are signed. Choose those leading left and continue west toward Little Si. Your route will lead around the base from south to north between the two mountains.

The two Si's are examples of different kinds of rock. Mount Si is old, slowly cooled magma from deep beneath the surface of the earth, called "gabbro." Little Si is volcanic rock that cooled more quickly, from beneath an oceanic lava flow, with telltale crystalline outcrops. Enormous old boulders have tumbled down the cliff separating the two peaks; the resulting rock slide is now covered by moss and shaded by firs and hemlocks. Look for a tiny log cabin with a mossy thatched roof, filled with rescue equipment and labeled "EMERGENCY SHELTER AND REST AREA." Children love peeking in and will want to stay in it because it is just their size.

The trail starts steeply up again on the west side of the mountain through salal and over rocky ledges. Some ledges come equipped with trees and branches just the right size for handholds.

At the summit a dry microclimate has encouraged pine and manzanitas to grow. As you rest, explain plate tectonics to your kids with visual aids. Tell them that the plate beneath the ocean shoves against the plate of the continent zone, and as a result rocks are crunched, folded, and "smooshed," and the oceanic plate dives under the continental one. Only after centuries of uplifting and erosion can we see the result. For the benefit of the children you may want to compare the chunks of different kinds of rock mixed together to the nuts, fruits, and batter in a fruitcake. The rocks have been lifted to the surface and eroded away, so we can see the tectonic action. In the mixture are hard and soft pieces—hard blobs as big as Mount Si, or as small as their fist—the fruit mixed into the cake of soft sandstone.

From the summit slabs, children can look out over the valley and across to Rattlesnake Mountain. (Assure them that no rattlesnakes live there or here.) The foothills below contain the Wilderness Rim subdivision and Rattlesnake Lake, the distant South Fork of the Snoqualmie, downtown North Bend, and the up-close meandering Middle Fork Snoqualmie. Now turn and gaze at the face of massive Mount Si behind you, close enough to breathe on. Tell the children that when they get a little older, that summit can be their objective.

32. Twin Falls

Type: Dayhike
Difficulty: Easy for children
Hikable: April–November
One way to top of falls: 1³/₄ miles
One way from
John Wayne trailhead: 3¹/₄ miles
High point: 900 feet
Elevation gain and loss: 300 feet
Green Trails map: No. 206 Bandera

This Washington State Park trail was rebuilt in late 1989, as compensation for a new hydroelectric project, the Weeks Falls power plant, farther up the river. The walk through magnificent old-growth forest leads to views of two South Fork Snoqualmie waterfalls. Children will love everything about this hike: the moss-covered nurse logs, the enormous cedar and fir trees, the panoramic view at waterfall level from a viewing platform, and the bridge crossing over and between two waterfalls. The wonder of falling water forming into spray, dropping, dropping, and then becoming river again holds timeless fascination for children of all ages.

With two cars it is possible (though not recommended) to make a one-way downhill loop. This option is described later.

 Drive east on I-90 to Exit 34 (the Edgewick Road) and turn right on 468th Avenue S.E. Continue 0.6 mile, turn left on S.E. 159th, and find a parking lot in another 0.6 mile at the road's end (elevation 600).

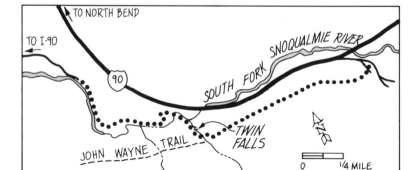

Beginning at the lower end of the trail, walk a graveled and graded surface past moss-covered second-growth alder and maple. As you follow the river, larger and older evergreens provide canopy. In a short mile the trail switchbacks 300 feet up a rocky moraine for a first view of the fan-shaped 90-foot lower falls, with a three-way trail fork. For

Giant fir tree alongside Twin Falls Trail

the best view, go right 20 feet. This makes a fine turnaround point, or return to the river's edge for a picnic.

To continue on, choose the central trail, leading down to the river. Once there, turn right off the trail beside a truly enormous old fir, perhaps 700 years old, and pause on the river's edge. Directly over everything hovers 1300-foot Mount Washington, clear-cut on this side.

From here the trail climbs again. The kids will love the side trip down a flight of 103 steps to a viewing platform opposite the falls. Families stand transfixed at the spectacular sight of the sculpted cliff covered by falling white water. Children can imagine they are suspended over the river, and look down at caves behind the falls that have been eroded by the water's force. The caves are frequently filled with branches and logs, held in place by the waterfall.

Back on the trail continue up a fern-covered ridge, at times within sound of the freeway, past enormous moss-covered gray blocks of basalt like Inca ruins. Reach the bridge over the top of the falls $1^3/_4$ miles from the lower parking lot. The bridge is substantial enough for the most timid; from here, stop to gaze at the powerful two-stage upper falls. Jagged gray boulders lined with maidenhair ferns channel the water first right, then left. For other impressive views, cross the bridge and walk $^1/_4$ mile to another enormous old tree where a family can munch and ponder the force of water.

One-way downhill option: While this may sound good, it does not save much energy, it involves a discouragingly long $^1/_2$ mile road walk, and you can't see the falls as you hike. For a one-way hike, leave one car at the lower parking lot, then return to I-90 and drive to Exit 38, Homestead Valley Road. At the end turn right, and in 0.1 mile turn right again into a large parking lot for the John Wayne Trail (elevation 900 feet).

Begin by walking west on the gated road. At $^1/_2$ mile, just short of an electrical substation, find the Twin Falls Trail. Descend another mile to the bridge above the falls, then continue down to the lower parking lot.

33. Commonwealth Basin

Type:	Dayhike or overnight
Difficulty:	Difficult for children
Hikable:	June–October
One way:	3½ miles
High point:	4200 feet
Elevation gain:	1300 feet in, 300 feet return
Green Trails map:	No. 207 Snoqualmie Pass
U.S. Forest Service map:	Mt. Baker–Snoqualmie

A popular timbered valley in the Alpine Lakes Wilderness offers families campsites high above Snoqualmie Pass with a multichanneled creek to explore and views of area peaks. Children can enjoy endless water games, and will love camping away from the sounds of the buses and trucks on the freeway.

My children thought Commonwealth Basin had the best frogs. We all remember how they collected several large croakers and threw them into my tent while I slept. But our memories of how I reacted have changed with the years: they say I screamed; I say I was only mildly amused. But I can still point out the campsite where they woke me from my nap with those clammy creatures, hopping in confusion. It wasn't easy to corral them and get them out of the tent.

Drive east on I-90 to Exit 52 at Snoqualmie Pass. (If you are coming from the east, use Exit 51.) Go north under the freeway and find the parking lot for the Pacific Crest Trail on the north side of the road (elevation 3000 feet).

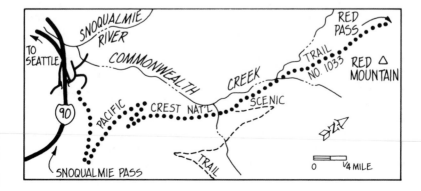

Commonwealth Basin meadow

Hike the Pacific Crest Trail northward in mature forest on long switchbacks, climbing to the 4200-foot high point in 2 miles. Views open up to the massive wall of Guye Peak, the other side of Alpental across the valley. From here the trail descends toward the creek, and at 2½ miles reaches a fork. A signed trail leads down into Commonwealth Basin (elevation 3900 feet).

A number of good family campsites are available in the next mile along Commonwealth Creek beside an avalanche slope sometimes still covered with down timber in early summer. The creek channel splits and meanders, providing bars and uncharted islands for children to explore.

The trail continues on up to Red Pass and stunning, dramatic views to the north. On a clear day expect to see Mount Rainier and perhaps Mount St. Helens and Mount Hood.

34. Thorp Mountain

Type: Dayhike
Difficulty: Difficult for children
Hikable: June–October
One way: 2 miles
High point: 5854 feet
Elevation gain: 1800 feet
Green Trails map: No. 208 Kachess Lake
U.S. Forest Service map: Wenatchee

A child's chance to climb to a former lookout tower and feel the responsibility lookouts felt surveying the forests for fires. This is a very steep trail, gaining an average of 900 feet a mile, so don't push your children if this elevation gain would be too much for them. The trail switchbacks through meadows to Kachess Ridge, crossing above little Thorp Lake to the lookout viewpoint. Expect to see Mount Rainier, Mount Adams, and Lake Cle Elum, counterpointed by deep green hills and rocky ridges. Be sure to carry water, as there is none.

Drive I-90 to Exit 80, Roslyn. Drive through Roslyn and Ronald on Road No. 903. Continue on, driving the length of Lake Cle Elum and passing a campground at Whish Poosh. (Children love this name. Have them say it quickly three times, then tell them it means "Big Beaver," one of the Indian gods.) Pass another campground on the Cle Elum River. At 11 miles from Roslyn, turn left on the French Cabin Creek Road No. 4308, cross the Cle Elum River, and drive 5 miles. Go right on Road No. (4308) 120, signed "KNOX CREEK TRAIL." Drive

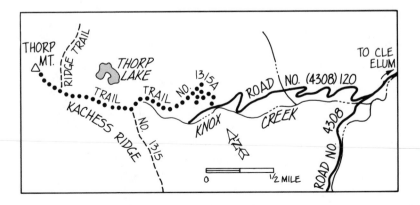

another 2 miles to the trailhead of Trail No. 1315 (elevation 4200 feet).

The trail switchbacks steeply up a south-facing meadow slope with several difficult steep spots. Springtime flowers are glorious, and July and August bring new and continuing blooms. In late July we were delighted by three varieties of penstemon in differing shades of pink and lavender, Mertens' bluebells, and two varieties of golden arnica. If your children know the story of *Heidi*, they will remember how the Swiss meadows helped heal her crippled friend Clara. Several rock outcrops make good sitting spots for energy snacks.

At the top of the meadows the trail contours left to Kachess Ridge (elevation 4000 feet). Turn right, dip a little, and follow the crest of the ridge another mile to a junction. Go left and climb steeply again to the lookout building, built in 1931 and perched on the highest crag (elevation 5854 feet). Stop to gasp at views down long, lovely Lake Cle Elum and tiny Thorp Lake directly below, to intermediate hills above the Teanaway Valley, and the giant snowy volcanoes beyond to the south.

Thorp Mountain Lookout

35. Esmerelda Basin

Type: Dayhike or overnight
Difficulty: Moderate for children
Hikable: June–October
One way: 3 miles
High point: 5400 feet
Elevation gain: 200 feet
Green Trails map: No. 209 Mt. Stuart
U.S. Forest Service map: Wenatchee

One of the wonderful aspects of the Teanaway River Valley (Indian for "Place of Fish and Berries") is the promise of sunshine. Though the weather may be cool and wet in Seattle, the Teanaway Valley, in the rain shadow of the Cascades, usually has dependable sunshine.

An old miners' access road to long-ago gold mines now switchbacks through flower-filled meadows to high viewpoints. Children will be intrigued by the sight of rock climbers with their curious gear, leaving from the same trailhead to climb Ingalls Peak. The trail is wide and gains elevation gradually between rugged ridges, past flower gardens renowned among botanists for their rare and unusual species.

Drive I-90 east to Cle Elum. On the eastern outskirts of town, bear left onto U.S. Highway 97. In 5 miles, turn sharply onto the Teanaway River Road. Continue, following North Fork Teanaway signs, to a junction in 13.5 miles at 29 Pines Campground. Go right, pass Beverly Camp, and at 23 miles reach the end of the road and the trailhead of Trail No. 1394 (elevation 4243 feet).

The distinctive pink-red cliffs of the Teanaway Valley are as fascinating to children today as they were to their grandfathers. If the kids' eyes are sharp, they may see tailings from miners' tunnels along

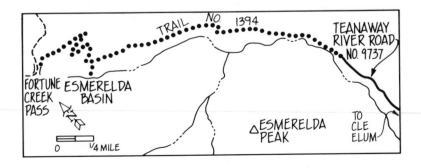

Esmerelda Basin trail

the base of the cliffs. Explain that the miners took samples of gold, silver, copper, and chrome ore from these mountains, but not in sufficient quantities to pay them a living wage. Instead, they took the samples to speculators who bought stock in the mines.

Begin steeply at first between Esmerelda Peak on the left and Teanaway Peak on the right, alongside rushing Esmerelda Creek. If a child can be lured up the first ¼ mile of this climb, the rest will be relatively easy. Switchback above the creek past several possible campsites (if you are on a first backpack with a baby, a camp along the river here would be a good choice), then gain elevation more gradually until ½ mile, where the trail splits to the right for Ingalls Way. Since the trail is an old road, it is wide enough for families to walk holding hands at the beginning. Continue past a swampy meadow filled in late June and early July with white bog orchids, hot pink shooting stars, and little red "elephant's heads." (Kids should look for the tiny elephants' uplifted trunks).

Rockeries filled with showy flowers improve in color and diversity with every step. The trail is steep and rough in places, and has numerous creeks in early summer, where young children will need help. An unmarked fork at 1¼ miles has logs barring one way. Go right and gauge the elevation you've gained by the cliffs and snow patches on the opposite wall. Look for lavender mats of creeping phlox, pink Indian paintbrush, scarlet gilia, and cream-colored pussy toes. (Have the kids look for the kittens' tiny paw pads.) Some rockeries have clumps of delicate *Lewisia columbiana* with a tiny pink stripe on each petal.

At 2 miles reach Esmerelda Basin, the site of an old gold-mining camp. Stop to look, munch, and enjoy. If you brought a map, pull it out to identify the peaks and ridges around you. If your family has sufficient energy, continue 1 mile more on easy switchbacks to Fortune Creek Pass for the satisfaction of reaching the high point and wonderful views of the Cle Elum drainage, Mount Hinman, Mount Daniels, and Cathedral Peak.

36. Lake Marion

Type: Dayhike or overnight
Difficulty: Moderate for children
Hikable: July–October
One way: 1½ miles
High point: 5500 feet
Elevation gain: 900 feet
U.S. Forest Service map: Wenatchee

Small, shallow Lake Marion is surrounded by fir and larch trees, with meadows and a rock slide at the end of a very steep trail. Because the lake bottom is sand, children can safely play in water warmed by summer sun. On a hot day even parents will want a refreshing wade. Try this hike in late September or early October, when the larch trees have a golden glow.

Children attempting this hike should be strong and accustomed to steep trails, as this one is a huffer-puffer, climbing 900 feet in 1 mile. The good part is the trail is short. The bad part is that it is open to motorbikes and horses.

Starting in Wenatchee, follow Wenatchee Avenue south and turn onto Miller Street, which angles off to the right. Turn left on Crawford, then right on Mission Road, which becomes Squilchuck. Approximately

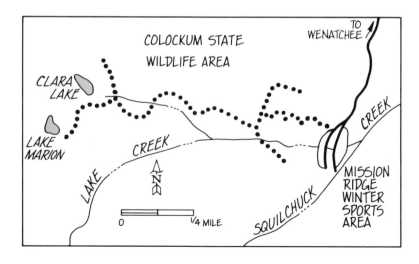

12 miles from Wenatchee, reach the edge of the large Mission Ridge parking area, and find the Clara Lake–Squilchuck Trail No. 1200 on the right side (elevation 4600 feet).

The trail starts steeply and stays steep, passing through a forest of fir and ponderosa pine. A confusing mixture of shortcuts and old trails might make you wonder if you are on the right trail. The trail alternates between forest and the rubble of an old lava flow, zigzagging upward. At $1/3$ mile look for an intersection; go left about 200 feet on an abandoned roadbed, then right on the trail again. Cross a creek at $3/4$ mile. Just before 1 mile the climb eases off; at $1 1/4$ miles look for a junction signed "LIBERTY–BEEHIVE." This trail leads to swampy Clara Lake. Go left, and in $1/4$ mile, after passing a marsh, arrive at little Lake Marion, gleaming in the sunlight.

Meadow flowers surround the shoreline, and there are two nice campsites, one on the right side of the lake and one on the left side, next to a hollow tree that looks like a guardhouse in front of a queen's palace. All it needs is a soldier in a red coat. While here, we came across a snowshoe rabbit in summer coloring, with a baby in her mouth.

Lake Marion

37. Nisqually National Wildlife Refuge

Type:	Dayhike
Difficulty:	Moderate for children
Hikable:	Year-round
Brown Farm Loop:	5½ miles
Ring Loop Trail:	½ mile
Nisqually Loop Trail:	½ mile
High point:	10 feet
Elevation gain:	None
Map:	Nisqually National Wildlife Refuge brochure

The Nisqually National Wildlife Refuge is a treasury of birds and wildlife at any time of the year, but children will especially love this hike in the spring, when ducklings, goslings, and baby rabbits are everywhere. The amazing colony of blue herons across McAllister Creek is on nests from mid-April through mid-June. Even seen from ½ mile away, the chance to watch the big birds swooping through the air to bring fish back to the nests for their babies is a special treat.

The mouth of the Nisqually was an undiked delta—mostly marshes and wetland—before nineteenth-century settlers tried grazing cows here. The farmers wanted to hold back the salt water, channel the creek, and provide road access around the farms, so, like the Dutch, they built dikes. The last of these farms—the Brown Farm—was sold to the U.S. Government in the mid-1970s to form the refuge. Now the river and creek are part of a national refuge, with few reminders of the earlier farms. The sounds of freeway traffic die away as you and the children hear only the sounds of birds—honks, quacks, and peeps—and peace. The Nisqually estuary is one of the few remaining undisturbed salt marshes in south Puget Sound. It is a nursery area for countless small plants and animals that, in turn, serve as food for birds and marine animals. The health of the salt marshes decides the survival of all the animals (fish, seals, birds) that depend on it.

Children may not want to walk the entire 5½-mile loop. It is too long for toddlers. But any portion can provide a stunning glimpse of an eagle, coyote, goldfinch, or cormorant.

Get off I-5 at Exit 114, go under the freeway, and double back to the Nisqually Refuge parking lot (elevation 10 feet). Pets are allowed only in the parking lot, and even there must be on a leash. Bikes, horses, and joggers are not allowed, and families are encouraged to

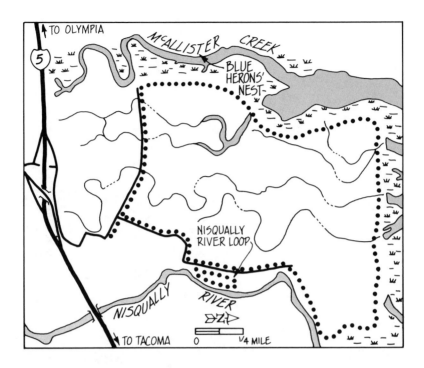

walk and talk quietly so as not to disturb wildlife. A $2 entrance fee for a family is required.

Start on the Brown Farm Loop through an old orchard in full bloom in early May. Children will feel they have entered an enchanted place. Pass a moss-covered cistern that looks like an ancient tomb. By turning left, or counterclockwise, you will reach McAllister Creek in only 1½ miles. Here the richness and diversity of ducks and shore-bird species will suggest to children that Noah just landed his ark here. We saw gadwall, goldeneyes, buffleheads, green-winged teal, shovelers feeding on surface plankton, American widgeons, mergansers, mallards, yellow legs, ruddy ducks, Canada geese, russet-colored horned grebes, and cormorants (the trained Oriental fishing birds in *The Five Chinese Brothers*).

But the high point was watching the wonderful colony of blue herons soaring, feeding, and nesting. The herons' wingspans appear almost prehistoric. Up and down the creek they flew—five and six at a time—now stopping to fish along the banks, now returning to their huge nests high in the Douglas firs and perching to feed their young. Tell children this is the bird equivalent of feeding a baby in a high chair.

Great blue heron nest

This entire trail is level and may seem tedious unless you see birds and animals. But if kids are quiet, they certainly will. Reach the first view of Puget Sound and the outside edge of the refuge at 2½ miles. Tidal salt marshlands beyond here are green hummocks above mud flats. Gaze out beyond the flats to the sound, back to Mount Rainier, then look over the dike for blinds where you can crouch to observe wildlife unnoticed. From the new Centennial Blind at 3⅔ miles we saw two eagles perched on a driftwood stump, waiting for the tide to serve their dinner.

Continue south along the swifter-flowing Nisqually River, pausing for two shorter trails. The Ring Loop Trail at 4⅓ miles leads ½ mile out into the delta and back to rejoin the main Brown Farm Trail. This trail can also be taken as a separate trip by going clockwise at the start of the Brown Farm Trail. The other short loop is the Nisqually River Loop—also ½ mile—which provides the closest short alternative trail in the refuge. Reach it by going counterclockwise from the parking lot. Children can't go wrong on any of them.

38. Green River Gorge

Type:	Dayhike
Difficulty:	Easy for children
Hikable:	Year-round
One way:	½, 1½, and 1 mile
High point:	800 feet
Elevation loss and gain:	300 feet
U.S.G.S. map:	Cumberland
Other maps:	King County road map, Thomas Map of King County

A surprisingly deep and beautiful river canyon, carved through soft sandstone by the Green River, lies within a thirty-minute drive from many points in the Puget Sound basin. Its appeal for families lies in the idyllic wilderness quality of the gorge itself. As you drop 300 to 400 feet down steep trails or steps to the riverbanks, you drop away from the sounds and compulsions of urban life. Children are fascinated by the walls, caves, pots, pillars, tunnels, and bridges carved into solid stone by the energy, force, and power of the water. The Green River originates on the Cascade crest at Green Pass on Blowout Mountain, many miles distant; passes over Howard Hansen Dam, which affects its flow volume; and ultimately empties into the Duwamish River. For a wonderful 10 to 12 miles its channel deepens into a gorge unlike anything else on this side of the Cascades. Three of the safer accesses are described.

Hike A: The top of the gorge can be accessed from Kanasket–Palmer State Park. From Renton take State Highway 169 east about 15 miles (11 miles north from Enumclaw) to the Four Corners Shopping Center, and turn north on the Kent–Kangley Road. In 3.5 miles turn right onto the Retreat–Kanasket Road. Continue on this road about 4.5 miles to reach Kanasket–Palmer State Park (elevation 850 feet).

The park has fifty campsites; many rafters and kayakers planning to float through the gorge to Flaming Geyser State Park put in here. Cliffs and canyon walls are just beginning to deepen. A pleasant 0.5-mile walk on an unpaved path from one side of the park to the other, along the Green River, rounds a big bend, where, because of a steep grade in the riverbed, the current is swift and you can see white water rapids.

Hike B: From Kanasket–Palmer State Park the river drops into an ever-deepening gorge near the Franklin Bridge, 5.3 miles down Enumclaw–Franklin Road. Take the cutoff signed "GREEN RIVER ROAD" for 2.5 miles. Go north 0.2 mile to the Green River Gorge Resort and the Franklin Bridge. The old resort has seen better days, but it still offers access to one of the best deep-gorge trails. The resort charges user fees of $2 per adult and $1 per child. (If this seems steep, so is the alternative: hiking 300 feet down a precipitous fisherman's trail without stairs or a railing.) But be sure to walk across the Franklin Bridge first to enjoy the beauty of the gorge from above.

From the resort, drop down steep flights of steps over a tributary waterfall to the gorge's floor. Just below the bridge the river narrows to a chutelike funnel. Immense molded mossy boulders rest on one side of the channel. Cross another waterfall on a plank, and find a tunnel sculpted through solid rock, leading out to a large, flat ledge above the river. The ledge has been scoured by high water and contains potholes, eroded by a single rock rotating round and round, much like those at the ocean. We watched two water ouzels dipping and dropping underwater here. Children can see why they are called dippers. Continue on the trail past river-carved level spots alongside another waterfall. These make good picnic sites or turnaround points. Look for old trees with their roots wrapped around boulders; they have thereby avoided being swept away by the current.

Hold on to children here. If they see rafters and kayakers paddling by, they may think they can jump in for a swim. The current is swifter than it appears to be, as an occasional large boiling bubble testifies. The trail continues through old cedars, stumps, and firs, some of which were burned by a fire sixty to eighty years ago. The cliffs on the opposite side of the river are deeply undercut: one more example of the effect of continuing river erosion.

When the trail abruptly turns straight up the side of the gorge at about 1½ miles, it is time to retrace your steps and coax children to go back. Along the way are any number of good play areas. Don't hurry back. This is a beauty spot unlike any other your children will see.

Hike C: An undeveloped and unsigned state park by the name of Hanging Gardens is the last recommended access to the gorge floor. To find it after leaving the resort, drive southeast back along Enumclaw–Franklin Road for 1.8 miles to the trailhead, a small pullout on the right, marked with piles of old rock and broken asphalt. To reach Hanging Gardens from State Highway 169, at the Four Corners Shopping Center, continue on State Highway 169 past Black Diamond and cross the Green River Bridge. At 1.7 miles from the bridge, turn left

Swimming hole in Green River Gorge

at 385th, then in 0.1 mile turn left again on the Enumclaw–Franklin Road. Go 3.3 miles from the bridge, to the trailhead.

Parking is limited. Don't let the lack of a sign dismay you. Once over an initial barrier, a well-traveled four-wheel-drive road leads from this access about 1 mile toward the gorge. A cyclone fence runs parallel to the road on the right side for much of the way, setting off private property. Continue down two short, steep drops (one consists of clay, which is slippery when wet) to the first view of the gorge and a campsite with a fire pit. A few hundred feet farther brings you to the river, a gravel bar, and a view of an 80-foot-high sandstone cliff with the hanging gardens. Small pockets of soil have clumped themselves onto promontories and projecting bulges on the sheer face of this opposite wall. Out of the pockets and cornices grow mosses, shrubs, and small trees, leaning and drooping toward the river. Former waterfalls may have scoured the walls. Horizontal hieroglyphics were carved when the sandstone was underwater. The rocky river beach delights kids.

Children can throw big rocks into the water to hear them splash, and small sticks to watch them spin in the current. There are whitewater rapids around the corner on either side of the beach, whose roar gives kids the feel of a wilderness river. As we sat on the beach munching and gazing at the garden wall, a pair of rafters drifted around the bend in the river. "However did you get here?" they asked in astonishment. Each of us had thought we had the river to ourselves.

Green River Gorge

39. Clear West Peak

Type: Dayhike or overnight
Difficulty: Moderate for children
Hikable: July–October
One way: 1½ miles
High point: 5643 feet
Elevation gain: 1000 feet
Green Trails map: No. 238 Greenwater
U.S. Forest Service map: Mt. Baker–Snoqualmie

A child's chance to climb a short steep mountain and exult that he is almost as high as Mount Rainier across the way. The trail is a ridge in subalpine timber surrounded by clear-cuts. Compare the ridge to the backbone of a dinosaur. The reward is getting to the top.

Drive east from Enumclaw on State Highway 410 for 21.8 miles; turn right (south) onto the West Fork Road No. 74. At 6.8 miles cross the West Fork of the White River, and Wrong Creek. At 8.2 miles go left on Road No. 7430, and drive another 7.3 miles to the end and the trailhead of Trail No. 1181 (elevation 4725 feet).

Step out of the car and look left or south over ridges clear-cut into a crazy quilt as far as the eye can see. Trail No. 1181 begins in clear-cuts and follows a narrow ridge with views back to the parking lot. (Kids can watch the car get smaller.) In July the fireweed, first flower to return after fires and clear-cuts, is a brilliant magenta. Enter subalpine trees at ¼ mile, with only an occasional window north into the Clearwater Wilderness. There are no glimpses of Mount Rainier to warn children of what is to come. The trail levels for brief respites, long enough to reassure kids that it won't all be up, up, up. Small chips of shale cover the narrow path in some sections—tiresome walking for little feet. The first switchbacks begin at 1 mile, and shortly you will see the first heart-stopping view south to Mount Rainier.

From this point on to the summit, expect to see penstemon, arnica, blueberries, lupine, and beargrass. Look down into the Clearwater Wilderness. Compare the amount of remaining old-growth forest with the clear-cut area, and decide whether we're doing a good job of caring for the Earth. There is so much to see in the last ¼ mile that the top comes almost as a surprise. If you bring water, you could camp on the flat summit, the site of an old fire lookout. When early morning light shades the Emmons Glacier pink-gold, your children may think

Summit of Clear West Peak and Mount Rainier

they are seeing the first-prize winner in the volcano division at the Puyallup Fair.

Look a long way to the north for the microwave tower. To the south, the panorama of Mount Rainier is dominated by the sheer mile-high cliff of Willis Wall, where you may see but not hear an avalanche of crashing ice blocks. To the left of the Emmons and Winthrop glaciers is the sharp spire of Little Tahoma.

Coming back down the children can watch the car get bigger again.

40. Goat Falls

Type:	Dayhike
Difficulty:	Easy for children
Hikable:	June–November
One way:	¾ mile
High point:	3140 feet
Elevation gain:	100 feet
Green Trails map:	No. 270 Mt. Rainier East
	(trail not shown)
U.S. Forest Service map:	Mt. Baker–Snoqualmie

This easy walk alongside a creek through a forested, V-shaped ravine leads past a series of small, tiered rapids, many just right for splashing in. The last one, Goat Falls, is only 10 or 12 feet: not a spectacular cascade by any standard, but exquisitely framed by a moss-covered cliff on one side and a steep, mossy bank on the other. Children can pretend they are following an enchanted trail left by Hansel and Gretel through the dark forest.

Drive east on State Highway 410 31.6 miles from Enumclaw and turn left on the Corral Pass Road No. 7174. In 0.6 mile go right on Road No. 7176 for another 0.1 mile, and left again at the sign for Goat Falls Trail No. 1189 into a driveway with a small, often-full parking area (elevation 3040 feet).

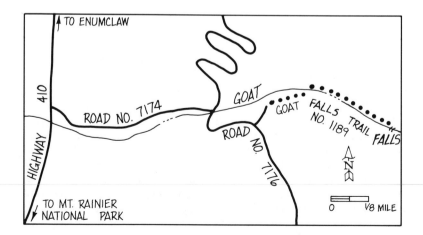

Goat Falls

As you step out of the car you may think that you have driven onto private property, where there could be no trailhead, but this is not the case. While the homes are private, the trail is public. Trail No. 1189 meanders between cabins for the first quarter mile. The old trees and steep ravine make this trail shady and cool even on a bright day. The trail climbs along Goat Creek, a series of small rapids between banks lined with twisted stalk, vanilla leaf, moss, and devil's club. Find a good resting place for a snack and a wading pool on a level bank at ¼ mile. Continue upward alongside a three-story boulder with overhanging balcony where small children may need help. At the trail's end is Goat Falls. On a warm day children can stand in the spray and enjoy the cool sprinkler feel of it.

41. Fremont Lookout

Type:	Dayhike
Difficulty:	Difficult for children
Hikable:	Late July–October
One way:	2¾ miles
High point:	7181 feet
Elevation gain:	900 feet
Green Trails map:	No. 270 Mt. Rainier East
National Park Service map:	Mount Rainier National Park Backcountry Planner

Hike to one of the few remaining high lookouts in the state, this one within Mount Rainier National Park. This hike offers children a glimpse of the life of a lookout and sweeping views of the north side of Mount Rainier, Berkeley Park, Grand Park, south Puget Sound, and the Olympics far beyond. The trip is especially interesting to children when the lookout is staffed. Check at the park's White River entrance before you start.

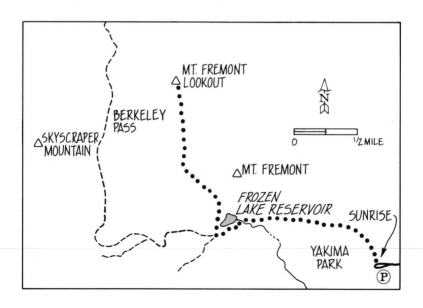

Fremont Lookout

Drive State Highway 410 east from Enumclaw to the White River entrance to Mount Rainier National Park and follow signs to Sunrise. Continue on up to the Sunrise parking lot (elevation 6350 feet).

From the visitor center, take the trail past the picnic area and climb very steeply up to Sourdough Ridge, keeping left at the fork near the top. Follow the ridge to Frozen Lake Reservoir, and a junction of five trails. Mount Fremont trail is the one on the far right, climbing a hillside to the north and gradually ascending through subalpine shrubs and flowers into the treeless true alpine zone.

For most of the way the trail is smooth, but with sections of natural cobblestones that can be troublesome for children. Trees are pruned down to mats by prevailing winds and snow loads, until they disappear entirely. Foresters have a name for a tree that develops

Marmot

shrublike qualities and has lower branches that sweep out like skirts. They call it a *krummholz*, (pronounced "crumb holts"). Your children may enjoy looking for trees that have become krummholzen and calling them by that crazy name.

Climb through rock gardens of pink heather, rose and cream paintbrush, tiny lavender alpine lupine, golden cinquefoil, and mountain wallflowers. Listen for the thunder of avalanches off Willis Wall and the shrill whistle of marmots heralding your approach. The trail reaches a 7300-foot high point, then descends to the lookout at 7181 feet.

Once at the lookout, gaze at the alpine meadows below in Berkeley and Grand parks, and the glint of Puget Sound and the Olympics far to the west. Children will want to talk with the ranger about life on a lookout. If the little building is empty, explain to your children that the ranger's main responsibility was to watch for smoke rising from a new forest fire, then to locate it with a complicated device called an Osborne Firefinder, and to radio in its exact location so that fire fighters could begin to put it out. Today surveillance planes have taken over most of that job, so rangers have more time to meet hikers and their families.

42. Boulder Cave

Type:	Dayhike
Difficulty:	Easy for children
Hikable:	June–November
One way:	¾ mile
High point:	2750 feet
Elevation gain:	300 feet, 100 feet return
Green Trails map:	No. 272 Old Scab Mountain
U.S. Forest Service map:	Wenatchee

Mother Nature sometimes provides unique treats for kids, and this is one of the best examples: a deep basalt gorge to explore, with a dark 200-foot-long cave/tunnel, so cold that on a hot day it feels like you're stepping into a refrigerator. The day we were there children from two families, ages three to twelve, were having fun listening to their echoes, exploring the tunnel, and throwing rocks into the pool. The last we saw of them they were happily investigating other caves. Boulder Cave is the official name, but since you can walk through it, you could easily call it a tunnel. Be sure your

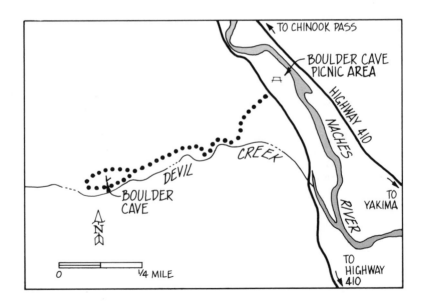

Boulder Cave Trail

family has a flashlight or, better yet, two or three, because the inside of the cave/tunnel is dark.

Drive State Highway 410 either east some 26 miles from Chinook Pass, or west 25 miles from the town of Naches. Between mileposts 95 and 96 turn onto a road signed "BOULDER CAVE NATIONAL RECREATION TRAIL." Drive 1.25 miles past a private campground to the trailhead (elevation 2450 feet).

Before starting out read the interpretive sign, which will help you explain how little Devils Creek formed the cave/tunnel. The trail starts directly behind the sign. (Don't confuse it with the paved nature trail loop leading to the river.) The way climbs gradually for ½ mile, levels off, and descends to a junction. Go either way, because this is the start of the loop trail through the cave, but the recommended direction is to the left, switchbacking 100 feet down to the level of Devils Creek, reduced to a mere trickle in summer. The trail enters the cave, where the tread is generally smooth, making an easy but dark passageway.

Bats live in this cave. In fact, they hibernate and nest here in the winter. Children probably won't see them, but the possibility that they may be sleeping nearby or could fly overhead adds to the cave's atmosphere. When this cave was discovered in the 1930s, it was thought to be home to more than a thousand Pacific long-eared bats, but by now, with tourists coming and going, there may be fewer than fifty. What do they eat, your kids may ask. Unlike vampire bats, which suck blood, these bats are happy to eat the insects constantly supplied to them by downdrafts in the gorge. How do they see in the darkness? Their eyesight is poor, but they use a form of sonar. The echoes of their high-pitched cries bounce off ceilings and rocky walls, and bats are able to navigate according to the echoes.

Proper and safe cave behavior includes no running, and being sure there is enough headroom before you venture inside. Have children experiment with the sound of their voices echoing against the walls. Words with vowels carry the best, and sometimes a simple "hello" will come back three or four times in quick succession. Try asking the question "Who are you?"

Don't hurry away. There are other small caves both above and below this one for children to explore safely.

43. Summit Lake

Type:	Dayhike or overnight
Difficulty:	Moderate for children
Hikable:	June–November
One way:	2½ miles
High point:	5439 feet
Elevation gain:	1100 feet
Green Trails map:	No. 237 Enumclaw
U.S. Forest Service map:	Mt. Baker–Snoqualmie

Lovely subalpine Summit Lake is set at the end of a ridge with a knockout view of the north side of Mount Rainier. Children will enjoy the gradual trail with its bridges over a creek and over an outlet from Twin Lake. Summit Lake has fish, and makes a wonderful place

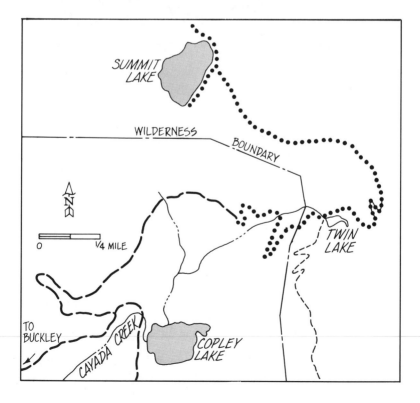

Summit Lake and Mount Rainier

for a high overnight camp with children if the cooking is done over a stove. Fires are not allowed, and camps must be more than ¼ mile from the shoreline. Fall camping is recommended because the insects are gone, and fall color and frosty mornings give children a sense of the coming of winter to the high country.

Drive State Highway 410 to a complicated intersection at the southeast corner of Buckley, and turn south on State Highway 162. Go 1.5 miles and turn left on State Highway 165, toward the Carbon River entrance to Mount Rainier National Park. Pass Wilkeson, Carbonado, and the one-lane bridge over the Carbon River. At 8.4 miles, at a Y-intersection, stay left on the Carbon River Road (the right branch goes uphill towards Mowich Lake). At 17 miles from State Highway 162, just before the Carbon River entrance to Mount Rainier National Park, turn left onto Road No. 7810 and cross the Carbon River. Stay on Road No. 7810 to its end and in 6.8 miles find the trailhead (elevation 4400 feet).

Begin in an old clear-cut, following switchbacks past subalpine trees coming up amid the stumps. Children may be glad to know that deer straying from the park into hunting areas outside it will have more protection as these little trees grow up. At ⅓ mile, cross a creek and continue into mature forest of very old alpine and noble firs. Enter the Clearwater Wilderness at ¾ mile. Look up at magnificent old trees and imagine what the area would look like today if citizens' efforts had not prevented it from being clear cut like the surrounding areas. The trail reaches a bridge over the outlet from Twin Lake (elevation 4750 feet) at about 1 mile. Where is the other twin? Most children love the fairy-tale quality of this little lake and bridge, and can imagine meeting the three Billy Goats Gruff. There is one good campsite here above the lake, which would make a turnaround point for a young family.

To continue on, follow switchbacks up the ridge leading to Summit Lake (elevation 5439 feet). For a great view of Mount Rainier reflected in the lake, follow the lakeshore trail to the right.

Flowers in August include lupine, beargrass, paintbrush, and false hellebore. There is swimming in ice-cold water for older children, there are small wading ponds for the younger ones, and for adults who think themselves lucky, there is fishing. As lovely as this setting is, parents should be prepared for onslaughts of mosquitoes until mid-August. The compensation is the alpine meadow setting for a jewel of a lake.

44. Chenuis Falls

Type:	Dayhike
Difficulty:	Easy for children
Hikable:	May–November
One way:	¼ mile
High point:	2200 feet
Elevation gain:	None
Green Trails map:	No. 269 Mt. Rainier West
National Park Service map:	Mount Rainier National Park Backcountry Trip Planner

Boulder hop across the bed of the Carbon River, stay steady over two single-file log bridges, and follow a brief loop path up to Chenuis Falls. Children will love the challenge of crossing the Carbon River, though some may need to be carried. A dip in the pool beneath the

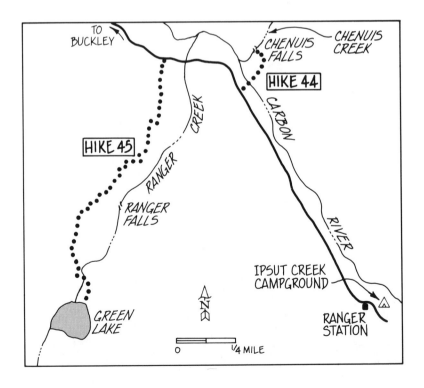

Crossing the Carbon River on the Chenuis Falls trail

falls is another incentive. The bridges often wash away during spring floods, so if the bridges are gone, take the children up to Green Lake (Hike 45) instead.

Drive State Highway 410 to a complicated intersection at the southeast corner of Buckley and turn south on State Highway 162. Go 1.5 miles, turn left on State Highway 165, and proceed 17 miles from here to the Carbon River entrance to Mount Rainier National Park, passing Wilkeson, Carbonado, and the one-lane bridge over the Carbon River. At 8.4 miles the highway goes uphill towards Mowich Lake; stay left on the Carbon River Road. Continue 3.6 miles past the entrance gate to the trailhead, which goes left across the riverbed (elevation 2020 feet).

The Carbon River changes its course annually, so the wide riverbed is filled with river rock, small streams, and pools to be navigated. Two logs with handrails cross the major volume of the glacial river water. Most children I observed loved making the crossings, but some commented, "Whew, I made it!" when they reached the other side. (Getting to the log bridges may require walking across loose and slippery river rocks; use caution.)

Once there, step into the shade of beautiful old-growth forest, with oak ferns and devil's club lining the path. Climb up alongside a prone giant fir and follow it to a fenced viewing point to see wilderness Chenuis Creek tumble into Chenuis Falls. The water does not drop vertically, but rather, within approximately 300 feet, drops 150 feet to a calm pool below. The hot day I was there families in swimsuits were playing in the pool and on the gravel bar below the falls.

45. Green Lake

Type: Dayhike
Difficulty: Moderate for children
Hikable: June–October
One way: 2 miles
High point: 3785 feet
Elevation gain: 1000 feet
Green Trails map: No. 269 Mt. Rainier West
National Park Service map: Mount Rainier National Park
Backcountry Trip Planner

A clear blue-green lake surrounded by forest and the steep cliffs of Arthur Peak and Tolmie Peak greets families at the end of this hike, but children will think the magnificent old-growth rain forest and Ranger Falls are reason enough to walk. The trail is easy to find, gets heavy use, and is eroded down to bony roots and rocks in some places, but it does gain its elevation gradually.

 Drive State Highway 410 to a complicated intersection at the southeast corner of Buckley and turn south on State Highway 162. Go 1.5 miles, turn left on State Highway 165, and proceed 17 miles from here to the Carbon River entrance to Mount Rainier National Park, passing through Wilkeson and Carbonado, and over the one-lane bridge across the Carbon River. At 8.4 miles the highway goes uphill toward Mowich Lake; stay left on the Carbon River Road. Find the trailhead 3.2 miles beyond the entrance, with a small parking place to the left and parallel parking allowed along the roadside. The trail is on the right (elevation 2020 feet).

Begin in a grove of giant true firs and Douglas firs that are centuries old. Their trunks are like tall pillars, and their size dwarfs small children. The forest floor is rich in oak fern, deer fern, and vanilla leaf. One gnarled root system (called a "root wad" by foresters), on edge beside the trail, could serve as a throne for a forest prince. Another root wad is 20 feet long and 12 feet high. Let the children stretch out their arms to get a sense of height and width.

Downed trees become nurse logs supporting rows of new hemlock trees, their tops waving like small green feathers. Some logs have fallen above the path like bridges to be walked under. At 1 mile, look and listen for the sound of water falling. A short descent brings you to the tiered cascade of Ranger Falls. The lower portion of the 100-foot waterfall splits into two falls. Children will want to linger here

Splashing in Green Lake

to feel the mist in their faces, and again above while crossing Ranger Creek on a log provided with railings. At this point the creek is wide and smooth, with pools children will want to explore. Wading is better here than in the lake, which is only ¼ mile or so farther.

Green Lake (elevation 3000 feet) is small and round with columnar cliffs rising steeply on opposite sides. Gaze up on a clear day toward Tolmie Peak, where fire lookouts survey their territory. As we ate lunch by the lakeshore, a Canada jay swooped down to beg nuts and raisins from us.

Note: Camping is not permitted here.

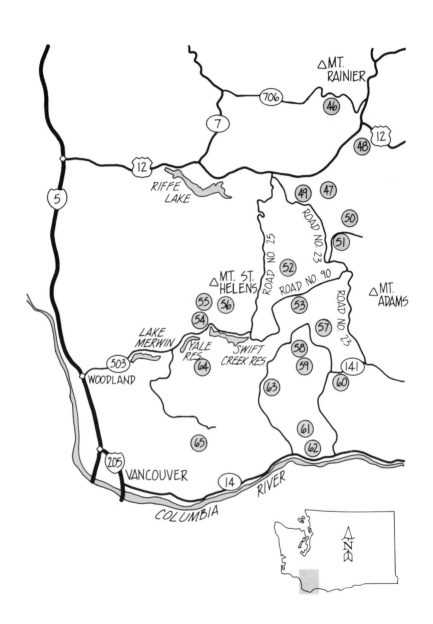

The South Cascades and Mount St. Helens

46. Snow Lake

Type: Dayhike or overnight
Difficulty: Easy for children
Hikable: July–October
One way: 1⅓ miles to Snow Lake,
⅔ mile to Bench Lake
High point: 4780 feet
Elevation gain: 340 feet in, 280 feet out
Green Trails map: No. 270 Mt. Rainier East
National Park Service map: Mount Rainier National Park
Backcountry Trip Planner

Another Snow Lake? A permanent snow patch may give this one the best right to the name. This child-delighting lake in Mount Rainier National Park is at the end of a short trail through subalpine meadowland. The lake has two campsites, a wading beach, and a permanent snow patch at one end where kids can slide and throw snowballs.

From the west take State Highway 7 south to State Highway No. 706. Turn east and drive to the Nisqually entrance on the southwest side of Mount Rainier National Park. Pass through Longmire and continue on uphill on the Longmire–Paradise Road. Two switchbacks above Narada Falls, turn right onto the Stevens Canyon Road. At 1.2

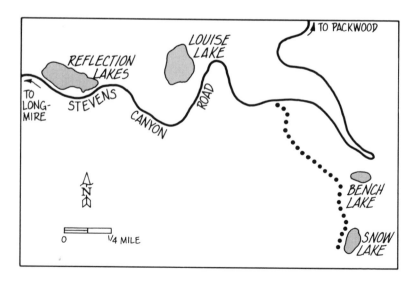

Jumping the inlet to Snow Lake

miles past Reflection Lakes find the trailhead (elevation 4520 feet).

The trail starts in a jungle of vine maple and willows, gaining 300 feet in the first ¼ mile. Children will need help on some of the giant steps the Park Service has built into the trail. The path levels off and enters flower fields punctuated with silver snags from a forest fire that swept through here seventy years ago.

A short side trail on a "hold-your-child's-hand" bluff gives an airy view of little Puddle Lake and larger Bench Lake. The trail loses most of the elevation gain, passing a side path to Bench Lake at 4542 feet. This is a possible turnaround point, but the lake is surrounded by heavy brush and has little to offer a child. From Bench Lake the trail continues its up-and-down ways, climbing again past a field of beargrass and great patches of heather, paintbrush, lupine, and little alpine trees, some small enough to be Christmas trees for mice.

The sound of Unicorn Creek flowing from the lake alerts you to the last climb, to the lip of Snow Lake. If you were lucky enough to get one of the two backcountry camping permits per day for this lake, take the trail across the creek to your campsite, located on a little finger of land. If you are dayhiking, continue on the trail along the shore of the deep blue lake to its shallow end, for wading. Since this is melted snow water, the wading is chilly, but most kids don't mind the temperature for short dips. On an August afternoon we found a frog, heard a marmot whistle, and saw a pika, while we ate lunch on logs. We looked up at the horn of Unicorn Peak and the fortresslike walls around the cirque. Waterfalls coursed down them to enter the lake. We continued the hike to the end of the lake to an avalanche snow slope. We found a gently tilted snowbank that made safe sliding for three little children with us. Then we turned around to discover the only view from the lake of Mount Rainier. The mountain had been watching over us all the time.

47. Cispus (Lookout) Point

Type: Dayhike
Difficulty: Moderate for children
Hikable: July–October
One way: 1¾ miles
High point: 5656 feet
Elevation gain: 1000 feet
Green Trails map: No. 334 Blue Lake
U.S. Forest Service map: Gifford Pinchot

Following an old Indian travel route up through a series of meadow ponds to a former lookout site will spell magic to a child. Be warned, the trail is *steep*. If you think the first part is steep, wait till you get to the last part! But at the trail's end, a child can feel on top of the world with views of Mounts Rainier, Adams, and St. Helens, the Goat Rocks, and the depths of the Cispus Valley. As a bonus, on the way back stop for a dip in a warm meadow pool.

Drive east from Randle on U.S. Highway 12. At 12.8 miles, just past the second turnoff for Beven Lake, turn left onto the Smith Creek Road No. 20. At a fork 4.3 miles from U.S. Highway 12, keep left. At 12.5 miles from the highway, pass the unmarked trail to Jackpot Lake and a possible campsite. At 12.7 miles reach the western trailhead

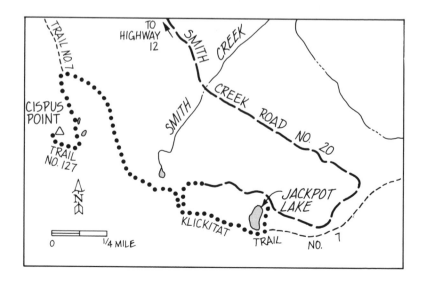

Castle Butte from small tarn on side of Cispus Point

(elevation 4600 feet), unmarked in 1991, of Klickitat Trail No. 7, leading to the Cispus lookout.

The way begins at the edge of a clear-cut, but shortly enters the refreshing shade of old-growth trees. After climbing 1 mile the trail emerges into ridge-top meadows. The way is part of the old Klickitat Trail, a former Indian pathway. Indian routes commonly traveled for miles on ridge tops, as this one does, because passage there was easier than in the denser forests below. Children can imagine they are Indians, carrying messages, trading goods, or joining distant cousins for a secret ceremony.

At an unmarked junction at 1.25 miles turn sharply left and start uphill again. Flowers become brighter in color and more showy as you ascend. Look for lupine, monkshood, pink paintbrush, false spirea, mountain azalea, and blueberries in August. Children may be more impressed with the patchwork quilt of clear-cut logging spread out on distant ridges like a giant checkerboard game. How would the scene have looked different to long-ago Indians? Once upon the summit, sit down for a bite and discover views stretching for hundreds of miles. Look down on the town of Randle, and listen for the sharp whistles of loggers' machines as they continue cutting trees in all directions.

On the way down, as we waded in one of the shallow, sun-warmed meadow ponds, we discovered a junco fluttering her wings and bathing with us.

48. Bluff Lake

Type: Dayhike or overnight
Difficulty: Moderate for children
Hikable: July–October
One way: 1½ miles
High point: 3841 feet
Elevation gain: 800 feet
Green Trails map: No. 302 Packwood
U.S. Forest Service map: Goat Rocks Wilderness

Swim or fish in a forest lake high in the Goat Rocks Wilderness. Since the bottom is muddy, there is no chance for wading, and small children should be careful. While we were there on a hot July morning, older children who were good swimmers were jumping from a large rock on the east shoreline into the deepest part of the lake. Bleached drift logs line one end of the lake and little children could sit on them and kick safely for water fun and games.

From Packwood, drive north on U.S. Highway 12 for 4.4 miles and turn right on Road No. 46. Drive 1.6 miles and go right on Road No. 4610. In another 1.5 miles the road makes a sharp right turn and becomes Road No. 4612. Views of the meandering Cowlitz River and Mount Rainier from this road are magnificent. At 5.6 miles from the

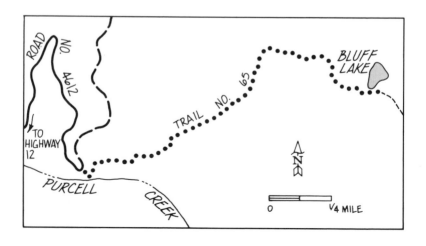

highway, reach the trailhead (elevation 3000 feet).

Head east along Purcell Creek and climb steeply up through hemlock and fir forest to reach the lake. Along the trail we came upon two tiny grouse chicks, only hours old, looking for their mother. The trail passes two rounded rocky balds, covered with moss but obviously of volcanic origin—perhaps the remains of an old lava flow. The lake is unmarked, and it is possible to walk by and miss it unless you are alerted by the sounds of splashing kids.

To get to the large rock campsite, continue another ¼ mile east past the first lake access. Small native trout can be caught here, we were told. Curling smoke from a campfire atop the rock looked like the signal from an Indian's camp.

Bluff Lake

Layser Cave

49. Layser Cave Interpretive Site

Type: Dayhike
Difficulty: Easy for children
Hikable: Year-round
Round trip: ¼ mile
High point: 1800 feet
Elevation loss: 100 feet
U.S. Forest Service map: Gifford Pinchot

This ancient Indian cave, used by long-ago Indian families for shelter and as a place to skin animal hides for clothing, will intrigue children. The age of the weapons found here make it one of the older archaeological sites in the state—perhaps 6000 years old.

From Randle, take Cispus Road No. 23 south for 7 miles. Turn left on a short spur road, Road No. (2300) 083, and drive 1.5 miles to the trailhead of Trail No. 290.

The trail drops to the right. Pause after 100 yards for a view of the Cispus Valley before going on to the cave. According to the Indians, everything on the horizon was named by Coyote. Look up to see Mount Adams, look over the Cispus Valley to Tongue Mountain, and across Juniper Ridge. Indians once drove deer and elk into a nearby steep box canyon, where they killed them with an atlatl, a dart shaft.

Continue on and down to Layser Cave, a natural 32-foot declining cave. Even on a hot day, when you enter the cave's mouth, it will feel cool, damp, and dark. Once inside, your eyes will adjust to the darkness. Picture Indian families sheltering here, making necklaces with shells traded from coastal Indians, and preparing hides for clothing. What would it have been like if fathers had not been able to find food for their families, you might ask children. They couldn't just go to the store, the freezer, or the cupboard for supplies. Would the families have gone hungry? Or moved on to another area? Bones of 108 deer were originally found here.

50. Hamilton Buttes

Type:	Dayhike or overnight
Difficulty:	Moderate for children
Hikable:	July–October
One way:	1 mile
High point:	5772 feet
Elevation gain:	800 feet
Green Trails map:	No. 334 Blue Lake
U.S. Forest Service map:	Gifford Pinchot

A stunning panorama of South Cascades peaks will reward families for this short steep hike. If you wish for a high campsite on a windless summer night, you could not improve on Hamilton Buttes. Picture moonlight and starlight on three icy volcanoes. A lookout once presided over this majestic scenery, watching for forest fires. Today airplane surveillance has replaced the lookout, but families who hike to this spot can pause, marvel, and enjoy the glorious view for as long as they wish. Carry water because there is none.

Your family may be unpleasantly surprised by the sudden appearance of a motorcycle on this high trail since it remains open to off-road vehicle traffic. Steep basalt cliffs on one side mean you should hold on to little children and watch older ones carefully. Despite these risks, this is one of the best hikes in the area, and will give a child a sense of beauty and accomplishment.

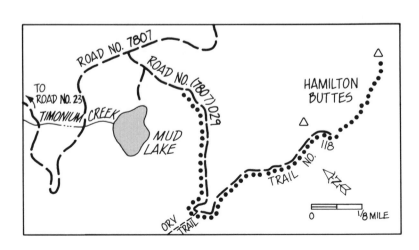

Mount Adams from Hamilton Butte

Drive 11.3 miles south of Randle on Cispus Road No. 23. Turn left
on Road No. 22 and drive 5.7 miles, then turn right on Road No. 78,
and drive 7.2 miles. Turn left on Road No. 7807 and drive 1.8 miles.
Turn right on Road No. (7807) 029 and drive 0.4 miles; pass Mud Lake
and find the trailhead for Trail No. 118 (elevation 5000 feet).

Begin walking upward through alpine trees on an old roadbed,
the way sandy with Mount St. Helens ash. At a fork at ½ mile keep
left—a bit farther the old road becomes trail. Switchback upward on
tread deeply rutted by motorcycle tires, through basalt outcrops and
alpine flower gardens to the summit. Children will feel suspended
between heaven and earth. Is this the highest point? A rock a bit
farther looks higher. Tell the children that despite appearances, the
other rock is not higher because you can see over its top.

Look south to Mount Adams, looming close enough for you to
inspect its snowfields and glaciers in detail. Beyond and farther south
is the faint silhouette of Mount Hood; westward is the gray, decaying
crater of Mount St. Helens. Look north to the enormous mass and
sweep of Mount Rainier, and east to the Goat Rocks, the oldest volcanic
formation in the 360-degree panorama. Listen to the sighing, whis-
pering, singing winds coming from every direction, and feel the peace
of this place.

Mount Adams and Takh Takh Lava Flow

51. Takh Takh Meadow and Lava Flow

Type: Dayhike or overnight
Difficulty: Easy for children
Hikable: July–October
One way: ½ mile
High point: 4650 feet
Elevation gain: 80 feet
Green Trails map: No. 334 Blue Lake
U.S. Forest Service map: Gifford Pinchot

Takhlakh Lake is the loveliest place in the Gifford Pinchot Forest, with its famous calendar-picture setting of Mount Adams reflected in the lake. The lake and popular campground are readily accessible by car. However, there are also two great trails. One, an easy 1-mile trail, circles the beautiful lake. The other, to Takh Takh Meadow, will fascinate 5- and 6-year-old children, as it climbs onto a 2000-year-old rough lava flow and weaves its way through lava solidified into chunks. Older kids will love to explore the rock crevasses and battlements like those on top of an ancient fort. Watch children carefully. The trail is excellent, but if you are exploring rock crevasses and battlements, parents should lead the way. Be sure you have plenty of mosquito repellent. The Takh Takh meadows are fine breeding grounds for these pests up until the beginning of August.

From the center of Randle, drive south, then east on Cispus Road No. 23 for about 32 miles; turn left on Road No. 2329 and go another 1.6 miles to Takhlakh Lake. The Takh Takh Meadow Trail starts at the campground. However, you can save 0.5 mile by passing the

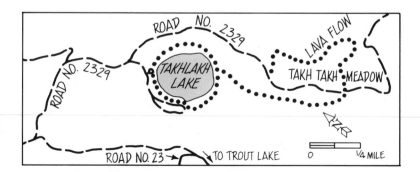

campground and driving another mile to where the signed trail crosses the road for the second time (elevation 4570 feet).

From the road the well-defined trail crosses the edge of Takh Takh Meadows. In mid-July have the kids look for elephant's heads, with their tiny trunks; shooting stars, with recurved petals shaped like a rocket blasting off; and cotton grass, with tufts like white cotton. Next the trail switchbacks steeply up what appears to be a rock slide but is actually the old lava flow. The Hawaiians have names for two forms of lava: the kind that cools slowly and is very rough (*ah ah*), and the kind that cools quickly, solidifies like a river in motion, and is smoother (*pahoe-hoe*). Ask the children which kind they think this is. It flowed downhill slowly, carrying huge chunks of solid lava that formed the great pile of rock that the trail climbs. Although the lava looks very recent, the trees growing on it show it is much, much older.

On top, the trail follows the lava flow downhill, passing the battlements and rock crevasses, finally descending into forest and at ½ mile reaching the road again. Either return the way you came or walk the road ½ mile back to the car. On a clear day magnificent Mount Adams will watch over you like a sentinel for the entire distance.

Takhlakh Lake and Mount Adams

52. Badger Ridge

Type: Dayhike
Difficulty: Moderate for children
Hikable: July–October
One way: 1 mile to point
High point: 5300 feet
Elevation gain: 400 feet
Green Trail map: No. 333 McCoy Peak
U.S. Forest Service map: Gifford Pinchot

Why Badger Ridge? Badgers are typically an eastern Washington animal, not seen in this area. Did a badger wander west of its normal range to give this ridge its name? More likely, the name giver mistook a marmot for a badger. Ask children which one they would rather meet on a trail: an ornery predator like the badger or a placid, meadow-dwelling, grass-eating marmot.

Whatever the name, this point is a high and lovely spot, well worth the drive and short walk. It is so remote that more elk than people use this trail. (Have the kids look for elk tracks.) At the saddle, youngsters can scan green parkland meadows and two volcanoes, then continue on to a rewarding destination. Older kids might also want to drop down to little spring-fed Badger Lake and to climb to the old lookout site, but there is a dangerous snow slope on the trail until late July, and so much soft pumice that the trail is not recommended for little children.

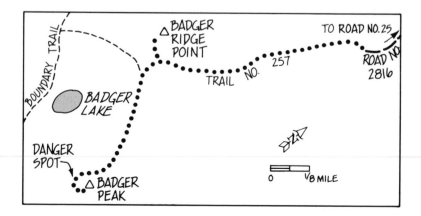

Drive south from Randle on Road No. 25. In 21 miles, or 2 miles south of Road No. 99, turn left onto Road No. 28. (From Woodland, drive County Road 503 to Yale—a service station. The road becomes Road 90. Follow it past the Yale and Swift reservoirs and the Pine Creek Visitors Center and continue on Elk Pass on Road No. 25. Continue 2.0 miles to Road No. 28.) At 2.7 miles from Road No. 25, turn right on a primitive road signed "BADGER RIDGE TRAIL." Drive another 4.5 miles to the trailhead of Trail No. 257 (elevation 4900 feet).

Begin walking in subalpine meadow on a sandy trail that drops and regains 100 feet in the first quarter mile. The cliff above and to the left almost seems to lean out over the soft sandy trail. Look over your shoulder to see whether Mount Rainier is still there. This is a good place to teach children to use a map and a landmark (Mount Rainier) to orient themselves. Can they find the four compass directions? Where will the sun come up tomorrow? Notice the numerous game trails that crisscross the path and the huge footprints. In a short mile the trail reaches a ridge top. Turn right on a fainter trail to Badger Ridge Point at the end of the ridge (elevation 5100 feet). Join the kids as they survey their kingdom. Plateaus and rocky tables clothed in bright green meadows spread between you and Mount Rainier and Mount St. Helens.

Where did all the pumice come from? Off and on for a thousand years, Mount St. Helens has spewed pumice, but soft hailstone-sized pumice showered down especially thickly in the 1980 eruption, covering everything inches deep. Although much has since washed away, the layer can still be seen on top of old stumps. Badger Peak was directly downwind from the mountain that day and got more than its share.

Late in July, when the snowbank has melted enough so that the trail is safe, if older children are determined to climb to the former lookout site, try it. Return to the trail, go over the ridge top, and descend steeply 500 feet to a junction. The right fork goes 1 mile more to Badger Lake; go left for the 5664-foot summit, where views are even grander because Mount Adams is unobscured. Early one morning we found a mountain goat there curled up like a dog, sleeping on the summit.

Mount Rainier from Badger Ridge

53. Middle Falls

Type: Dayhike
Difficulty: Easy for children
Hikable: Year-round
Loop trip: 1 mile
High point: 1800 feet
Elevation loss and gain: 250 feet
Green Trails map: No. 365 Lone Butte
U.S. Forest Service map: Gifford Pinchot

The South Cascades are second only to the Columbia River Gorge in boasting some of the most impressive waterfalls in the state. This easy loop trail includes views of two of these waterfalls from every possible vantage point. Families can gaze together at the beauty of Copper Creek and the Lewis River as they break loose and plunge freely, then regain their fluid composure. Kids love walking downward alongside the waterfall, being sprayed and deafened as they follow its course.

   Drive either south on Forest Road No. 25 from Randle or north on Road No. 90 from Cougar to the Pine Creek Information Center at the head of the Swift Reservoir; turn west on Road No. 90. At 14.5 miles from the information center, cross the Lewis River on a concrete bridge, and in another 3.3 miles enter the Middle Falls parking area (elevation 1800 feet). Because of the opportunity for a side trip, go clockwise on Trail No. 83.

At the far end of the parking area find the trail that goes to Copper Creek. Start by dropping steeply through old-growth trees to cross a bridge over the top of the first waterfall, Copper Creek. The trail contours around, still dropping, to a viewpoint across the ravine,

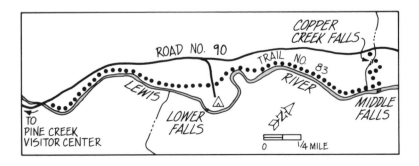

Middle Falls on Lewis River

and back up at the stream of white water coursing over a ledge from below the bridge just crossed. At ½ mile turn left on a fork and continue the descent to the level of the Lewis River.

The Middle Falls wrap around a projecting rock like a curtain around the prow of a ship. Children stand immobilized and hypnotized by the waterfall. Benches allow a family to sit and enjoy the view and the cool spray. The trail along the river provides more rapids and pools before climbing back to the car. Children can throw sticks and branches or launch leafboats, then watch them swirl and be swept away in the current.

If your family would like to continue to the Lower Falls along the Lewis River, you have the option of letting some of your party continue on the trail 1¼ miles while others climb back to the parking lot to drive the 1.2 miles to the Lower Falls Campground and trail access for a pickup point.

54. Trail of Two Forests

Type: Dayhike
Difficulty: Easy for children
Hikable: April–November
One way: ½ mile
High point: 1900 feet
Elevation gain: 80 feet
Green Trails map: No. 364 Mount St. Helens
U.S. Forest Service map: Mount St. Helens National
Volcanic Monument handout

Nature trails are usually a bore for young children. But someone, 1900 years ago, must have had kids in mind when a lava flow from Mount St. Helens covered a forest and created an 80-foot tunnel just big enough for kids between the ages five and fifty to crawl through. The Trail of Two Forests winds through an existing forest to lava casts of one that stood here 1900 years ago, so children can easily see the reason for the name of this trail.

 From Randle, drive south on Road No. 25. Turn west on Road No. 90, and go to Road No. 83 at the south end of Swift Reservoir. Turn left on Road No. 8303, and go another 0.2 mile to the Trail of Two Forests Picnic Area and trailhead (elevation 1700 feet). From the south, turn off I-5 at the Woodland exit and go north on State Highway No. 503, which becomes Road No. 90 past the town of Cougar. At 7 miles from Cougar, at the south end of Swift Reservoir, turn left on Road No. 83 and in 1.7 miles, turn left on Road No. 8303. Go 0.2 mile to trailhead.

The Trail of Two Forests starts from the parking lot, close to the restroom. The trail is a boardwalk level enough for strollers and wheelchairs. Interpretive signs explain that a "recent" lava flow covered a living forest. The intense heat from the molten lava consumed the wood, and the lava took the shape of the living trees. In some cases the trees were standing when the lava hardened, leaving deep, vertical wells. When the lava covered trees lying on the ground, they burned, leaving horizontal, pipelike tunnels. Many of the tree wells and partially formed tunnels are visible from the trail to intrigue and tantalize children into exploring them.

By a lucky chance, one of the tree wells leads to a tree tunnel, which leads to an opening 55 feet away, which leads to a bunch of happy kids crawling through it. Rangers say they pop in and out of the holes like chipmunks.

Exit from lava tube

A word of caution. Crawling through the lava tunnel is hard on knees and guaranteed to get hands and pants dirty. Warn your kids that shorts will leave their knees exposed, so be sure they wear long pants. It is dark—very dark—in the tunnel, with only a tiny light a long distance ahead. I recommend that a parent crawl through first to determine whether it is suitable for his or her children and perhaps to lead the way. (If you can manage a tiny flashlight while crawling, all the better.) You might as well see it for yourself, because your children will talk about their adventure for a long time.

55. Ape Caves

Type:	Dayhike
Difficulty:	Easy for children
Hikable:	March–November
One way:	¾ mile
High point:	2000 feet
Elevation loss and gain:	100 feet
Green Trails map:	No. 364 Mount St. Helens
U.S. Forest Service map:	Mount St. Helens National Volcanic Monument handout

"Hey Mom! It's the secret hiding place of a slime mold!" said the delighted little boy as he descended the steps into the cave. Another child said with a gleeful smile, "Now we're inside the volcano!" Of course she wasn't, but these are the longest intact lava tubes in the United States, visited by 96,000 visitors each year, and representing volcanic activity of Mount St. Helens perhaps 2000 years before the 1980 eruption.

Children will be disappointed when they hear how the Ape Caves got their name: they were discovered in 1951 by members of a mountaineering club called the Mount St. Helens Apes. No, there are no Bigfoot apes found there.

But the kids will be intrigued by the adventure of exploring the caves with a flashlight and learning how they were formed. Explain that lava tubes form in flows of ropy, molten basalt when the cooling lava forms a crust, just as a hot fudge sundae cools and forms a crust. At the end of the eruption, lava drained from the tube, leaving an open tunnel. For a simplified geological explanation of formation of the caves, look at the interpretive sign at the tunnel opening.

 Follow the directions for Trail of Two Forests (Hike 54). Pass the Trail of Two Forests, and at 2 miles from the junction of No. 83 turn right into a large parking lot and visitors center. If you didn't bring a big flashlight, lanterns may be rented here. Take jackets too, because it is very cold in the cave.

The cave is divided into two parts. The upper section is extremely rough and not recommended for children, but the lower section, described here, has a fairly smooth sand floor, and children find it exciting, safe, and easy going. The cave wind is caused by differences in air temperature inside and outside the cave.

Walk the paved trail 500 feet to the entrance of the lower cave.

Descend a flight of stairs into the cave, enter, and descend another flight to the main chamber. One can choose to walk ¼ mile, ½ mile, or all the way to the cave's end (¾ mile). Any distance will be interesting.

Note the shapes that the molten lava took when it solidified, and feel the texture of the walls. Ledges along the walls mark stages as the lava declined in the tube. Look upward for a "lava ball" wedged into the ceiling in a groove. This was a block of solidified lava that was carried along in the lava stream, then became wedged in a narrow portion of the passage 12 feet above the floor as the flow receded. Children who know *The Hobbit* will expect to hear Gollum's voice saying, "Not here, my precious!" To experiment with total darkness, turn off your lights when you are alone underground. Children may be surprised at how much darker the blackness of underground can be. Even starlight is missing.

Entrance to Ape Caves

56. Lava Canyon

Type: Dayhike
Difficulty: Easy for children
Hikable: June–November
One way: ½ mile
High point: 2900 feet
Elevation gain and loss: 300 feet
Green Trails map: No. 364 Mount St. Helens
U.S. Forest Service maps: Gifford Pinchot,
Mount St. Helens National
Volcanic Monument handout

Wonderful Lava Canyon was formed by an early eruption when Mount St. Helens poured out lava instead of pumice. Later a stream began to flow through the lava, eroding and excavating a twisting canyon. The 1980 eruption swept the canyon bare again, scouring the rock and taking out all vegetation and soil. Children will want to examine the walls of the canyon, formed by a combination of St. Helens eruptions. The water is too wild to play in, but young and old alike will be impressed with the deep canyon, raging water, and waterfalls. Hikers can cross the canyon on a bridge above the twisting torrent of white water, and pause to examine the water-sculpted basalt directly below. This paved new trail offers accessibility not only for those in wheelchairs, but also for those pushing strollers. Benches and viewing platforms have been placed strategically too, so you can sit and enjoy the rush of water and the breeze blowing up the canyon.

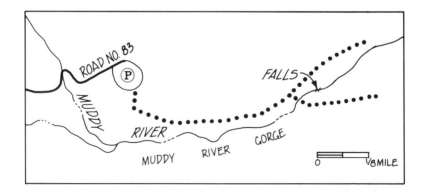

Lava Canyon trail

Following the directions for Trail of Two Forests (Hike 54), go to
the south end of Swift Reservoir. Turn uphill on Road No. 83 and
follow it approximately 10 miles to the Lahar Viewpoint, then a bit
farther to the Lava Canyon parking area.

Find the trail near the restroom and drop a few hundred yards
under old-growth trees to the level of the stream. Look at the water
and ask kids why this is called the Muddy River. Talk about where
the mud comes from. A series of switchbacks leads you down and
down the easy trail along the canyon. At the lowest level of the paved
trail, the canyon walls are of columnar basalt, dark gray against the
golden rock beside it. Below this point, a 1-mile loop trail continues
along blasted rock and dirt through the dangerous and exciting canyon. Too hazardous for little children, but perhaps they can follow it
another day when they are older. For now, however, go right on the
return section of the loop. The trail is safe enough as far as the steel
bridge over the raging stream.

57. Langfield Falls

Type: Dayhike
Difficulty: Easy for children
Hikable: Year-round
One way: ½ mile
High point: 3505 feet
Elevation loss and gain: 100 feet
Green Trails map: No. 366 Mt. Adams West
U.S. Forest Service map: Gifford Pinchot

The trail to this exquisite fan-shaped waterfall is an easy walk for young children. The trail begins above the falls and switchbacks down to its plunge pool, which is shallow enough for children to play in. On the way back up, take a side trail out to a stunning overlook of the top of the cascade.

From Trout Lake, go west on State Road No. 141 past the Mount Adams ranger station. Turn right on Road No. 88 and drive 14 miles to Tire Junction, a local landmark with a huge tire in the center of the road. Keep right on Road No. 88 for 0.1 mile and find the Langfield Falls Trail on the right (elevation 3505 feet).

Begin on a gentle descending trail, bypassing the first trail leading to the right (leave it for the return). At the midway point, find a bench and sign explaining that the falls were discovered by and named for K. C. Langfield, a Mount Adams ranger from 1933 to 1956, who loved

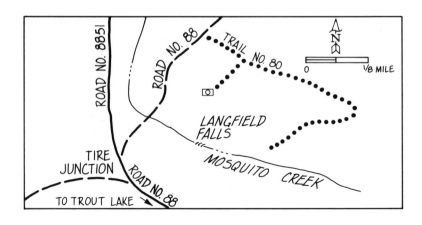

Langfield Falls

this beautiful spot. Next, kids can look for a hollow log with a porthole or foxhole on one side. Ask them who might use the hole.

Mosquito Creek tumbles 110 feet over a wide conglomerate wall. Small round rocks are embedded in the basalt; the pool basin is also rocky. Except at meltwater flood stage, the current is gentle, and children can soak their feet, wade, or throw pebbles and sticks into the stream. On the way back up, be sure to take the short side trip to look over the top of Langfield Falls. Imagine how you might feel if you were paddling your canoe along this stream, and came without warning upon the falls just ahead!

58. Placid Lake and Chenamus Lake

Type:	Dayhike or overnight
Difficulty:	Easy for children
Hikable:	Late June–November
One way to Placid Lake:	½ mile
One way to Chenamus Lake:	1½ miles
High point:	4245 feet
Elevation drop to Placid Lake:	60 feet
Elevation gain to Chenamus Lake:	160 feet
Green Trails map:	No. 365 Lone Butte
U.S. Forest Service map:	Indian Heaven Wilderness

Two warm, shallow woodland lakes await at the end of a short, level trail in the Indian Heaven Wilderness. Good wading beaches will appeal to children, and camps are available in the meadows surrounding both lakes. But because they are so close to the road, they get heavy use; best not to count on finding a campsite, but rather enjoy either or both lakes as dayhikes with your children.

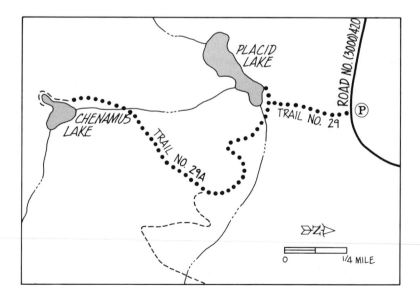

Chenamus Lake

 You can reach this trail from Indian Berry Fields by Road No. 24 and Road No. 30. To reach this trail from Carson, drive some 30 miles to the end of the Wind River Road. Turn right on Road No. 30, signed "LONE PINE," drive 2.3 miles, then turn right again on Road No. (3000) 420. Go another 1.2 miles to a large parking lot—usually crowded— and Trail No. 29 (elevation 4100 feet).

Begin on a wide, level trail under shady old-growth trees, undergrown with such plants as beargrass, vanilla leaf, and tiny wild strawberries. Placid Lake comes up quickly, and you will find kids taking off their sneakers before you can say a word. Wading is a little muddy in the shallow lake, but children love it anyway. The morning we were there, two rangers were having an earnest talk with a group of older kids about the "limits of acceptable change" in terms of campers' abuse of campsites. Campers with hatchets had been hacking living trees, damaging them severely, for no apparent reason. (The young people looked abashed, though not one held a hatchet.) Maybe people who like to chop need to be provided with chopping posts, like cats who need scratching posts.

Take a sharp left at an unsigned fork at the Placid lakeshore to continue on the trail to Chenamus Lake. At another fork marked for Trail No. 29A, go right. Cross three small creeks on stones, the last of which can be a difficult crossing during snowmelt. (For this reason the Chenamus trail is recommended for midsummer.) In another ¼ mile the trail levels off and the lake comes into view. The best wading and best campsites are here. Follow a trail around the lake to a small inlet for a pretty view. Chenamus is filling in with reeds, which attract dragonflies and hummingbirds. We saw a salamander swimming underwater (the kids would have envied his technique), and a mother duck followed by a convoy of five fat balls of fluff.

59. Junction Lake

Type: Dayhike or overnight
Difficulty: Moderate for children
Hikable: July–October
One way: 2½ miles
High point: 4730 feet
Elevation gain: 700 feet
Green Trails maps: No. 365 Lone Butte,
No. 397 Wind River
U.S. Forest Service map: Indian Heaven Wilderness

A warm, shallow wilderness lake surrounded by subalpine mead-ows, Junction will please families because there are a number of small ponds to lure kids with along the way. What is the junction? Its name evidently comes from the connection of this trail with the Pacific Crest Trail at the far end of the lake.

From Trout Lake, drive west on County Road No. 141 and pass the Mount Adams ranger station. At the Skamania County line the road becomes No. 24. Follow signs for "CARSON" and "BERRY FIELDS." At the first major junction, go straight ahead, following pavement onto Road No. 60. Eleven miles from Trout Lake, go north on Road No. 6026 for a few feet, and then straight ahead onto Road No. 6035. Find Trail No. 48 at 4 miles from Road No. 60 (elevation 4070 feet).

In ¼ mile step into wilderness and feel and smell the difference. Nothing has been cut down, graded, or gouged with motorcycle tracks. Children will like searching the lichen-encrusted tree trunks to see old men's beards, mustaches, and eyebrows in their shapes. The trail is wide and gains elevation gradually. There is some evidence of volcanic

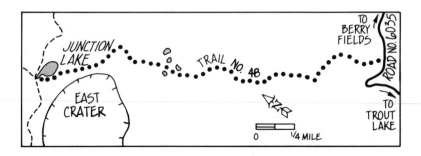

Junction Lake

 activity. To the left the tree-covered hill is a small dead crater, without a trail, and the little ponds along the ridge top between 1 and 2 miles are volcanic potholes. The potholes have mud bottoms, and some are filling in with grass and reeds, but they provide wading-pool-size places where children can stop and play or turn around.

Continue, and at 2½ miles drop slightly to find Junction's shore. The lake is probably too shallow for fish, but in midsummer it is just the right temperature for kids to play in. (Some like to stretch out prone, resting on the bottom, to pretend they are beached whales.) Camps around the edge of the lake have meadow and tree settings. If you stay, you may see the animals who come to drink in the evening or early morning.

60. Ice Cave and Natural Bridges

Type:	Dayhikes
Difficulty:	Easy for children
Hikable:	Year-round
One way to ice cave:	⅛ mile
One way to bridges:	⅛ mile
High point:	2900 feet
Elevation gain:	None
Green Trails map:	No. 388 Willard
U.S. Forest Service map:	Gifford Pinchot

Two lava tubes formed by long-ago Mount Adams lava flows resulted in fascinating play areas for kids. The first, an ice cave within a collapsed lava tube, contains ice stalactites and drip ice masses that last all

Ice Cave

summer long. Kids climb around on the ice in semidarkness, calling out to one another, "This place is awesome." The second is a pair of nearby natural bridges the family can walk over. The arched bridges are all that remain of more lava caves, whose tops have collapsed inward into a basalt basin.

 From Trout Lake go west on County Road No. 141. Pass the Mount Adams ranger station. At the Skamania County line the road becomes No. 24. At 6 miles from Trout Lake, turn left on a tiny dirt road and

Natural Bridge

go 0.2 mile to the ice caves. Back on Road No. 24, continue another 0.8 mile, turn left, and go 0.5 mile, then turn right to the Natural Bridges (Big Trench) parking area.

The ice cave has been known and used for almost a century. At one time, before freezers, the ice in the cave supplied the towns of Hood River and The Dalles. One end of the cave traps and holds moist, cold air, which settles during winter, then forms into ice columns, stalagtites, and pools. Temperatures have warmed up since the turn of the century, and it is hard to picture the cave's present ice supplying two towns' needs today. What it does supply is excitement for kids. On a hot day they descend a flight of stairs with flashlights in hand and their eyes grow wide in disbelief. "I'm gonna get me some ice to keep," they say. The cave recesses extend beyond the main room to a wind vent and a narrow tunnel exit on the other side of the parking lot.

A half mile farther down Road No. 24, turn left on Road No. 24 (041). Find a trailhead to the Natural Bridges. Walk 300 yards to a dry rocky basin spanned by two arches of bubble-filled basalt. Trails cross both of them, to the joy of children. If you doubt the bridges can support your weight, take note of the size of the tree trunk growing on top of one of them.

One can speculate about the river of lava that came through eons ago. Did its surface freeze on the top before the rest had cooled and solidified? When did it collapse inward? At both ends of the basin, find caves with roofs that the trail crosses over. In another thousand years will more natural bridges be here? Kids don't spend much time wondering. They like to run across, then turn and walk slowly to the middle, kneel, and peer down beneath the bridge to see what they can see beneath. Some like to play at being trolls to scare others crossing over.

61. Grassy Knoll

Type:	Dayhike
Difficulty:	
The Knoll:	Moderate for children
Grassy Knoll:	Difficult for children
Hikable:	March–November
One way:	
The Knoll:	1½ miles
Grassy Knoll:	3 miles
High point:	
The Knoll:	3610 feet
Grassy Knoll:	3648 feet
Elevation gain:	
The Knoll:	800 feet
Grassy Knoll:	1000 feet in, 200 feet out
Green Trails map:	No. 388 Willard
U.S. Forest Service map:	Gifford Pinchot

This large, rounded, meadowy knoll offers supreme views of the Columbia River and Mount Hood to the south, and of Mount Adams with its enormous old lava flow to the east. Children feel happy and excited about reaching the site of an old lookout on what used to be part of the Pacific Crest Trail. Their summit exhilaration is tempered into awe, however, by the majesty of the view.

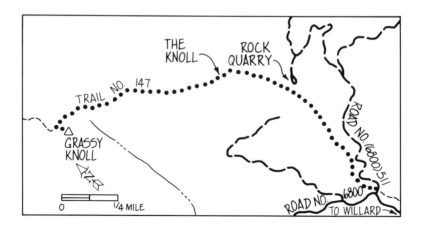

Mount Adams from "The Knoll" on Grassy Knoll trail

The trailhead can be reached from the west from the Wind River Highway by way of Road No. 6808 and Road No. 6800, or as described here from the east. Drive State Highway 14 east past Carson and turn north on Road No. 66. Pass through the small town of Willard. In 2 miles turn left on Road No. 68 (unsigned in 1991), go 7.2 miles, and then turn right on Road No. (6800) 511 for a few feet to Grass Mountain Trail No. 147 (elevation 2830 feet). (To reach another access that saves 1 mile of trail and 500 feet of climbing, follow Road No. (6800) 511 another 1.2 miles, then turn left on a service road and go 0.2 mile to the road's end in a rock quarry. Find a route through the quarry up to the trail.)

From the main trailhead, begin with a short walk in grassy meadow, then enter steep, wooded switchbacks. The forest is filled with tigers and princes—tiger lilies and prince's pines. This trail is steep for kids; lures and inducements such as candy and fruit are appropriate here. At 2900 feet and 1 mile, pass the old rock quarry. Next pass the burned remains of a clear-cut and at 1½ miles reach a basalt summit. Called simply "The Knoll," it is dominated by a fine view of Mount Adams and makes a good turnaround point.

But of course this is not the *Grassy* Knoll. From "The Knoll," the trail descend into forest with a carpet of moss, beargrass, lupine, and a few more tigers. It dips and rises for another ½ mile until a distinct barren rock appears on the horizon. As you approach it, the knoll shows its grassy rug. Climb for ¼ mile to the site of the old lookout, distinguishable by a bit of broken glass and foundation posts. The views south are down the Columbia River, over Dog Mountain to Mount Hood, and east to Mount Adams, which often wears a cap of clouds. Most of the rolling foothills are forested, with only a few clear cuts. Have the kids listen for the sound of boat horns on the river. Tiny plants blowing in the wind on the summit include phlox, yarrow, wild onion, and gray lichen. Like all "bellyflowers," they bear close examination. Time stands still in this lovely place.

62. Dog Mountain

Type: Dayhike
Difficulty: Difficult for children
Hikable: March–December
One way to first viewpoint: 1 mile
One way to lookout: 2½ miles
High point: 2940 feet
Elevation gain to first viewpoint: 1000 feet
Elevation gain to lookout: 2900 feet
Green Trails map: No. 430 Hood River
U.S. Forest Service map: Gifford Pinchot

This entire mountain is too long and steep a trip for little children, but the lower part of it provides splendid views of the Columbia River and the magnificent Columbia Gorge. Older children will find the entire climb an adventure with a payoff of a 30-mile view of the Columbia River and its canyon. Gaze east to sailboards fluttering like butterflies between Hood River and Stevenson. Look down on toylike open barges loaded with grain, some from as far upriver as Idaho. Small children will ooh and ah at the sight of tiny trains far below, winding up and down both sides of the river on miniature tracks.

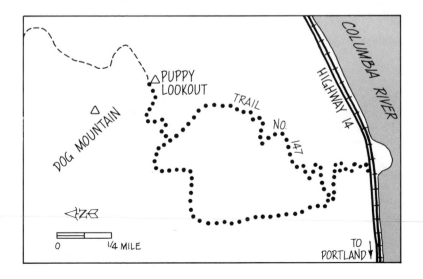

Columbia Gorge from Dog Mountain Trail

Listen for the lonesome sound of their whistles.

Don't push the children on this trail. It climbs 1000 feet in 1 mile—steep even for an experienced hiker. Poison oak and snakes can occasionally be found on this trail.

Drive State Highway 14 about 18 miles east of the Bridge of the Gods. Pass Stevenson and in another 9.5 miles (between mileposts 53 and 54), find a large parking area on the left side of the highway (elevation 186 feet). Find the Dog Mountain Trail No. 147 at the east end of the parking lot.

Trail No. 147 starts out gently, but quickly turns steep and rough, switchbacking relentlessly upward. Tempting glimpses through trees encourage one to go on. In a little over ½ mile you reach a junction;

go right. While the trail moderates a bit, it is still steep.

The trail continues up through forest carpeted with Oregon grape that has grown back since a pre-1950s fire. In late May and June look for spectacular stands of white ghost orchid. Only two switchbacks after emerging from the forest you will find the first great view of the Columbia River, 1 mile from the highway and a gain of about 1000 feet (elevation 1160 feet). Any child who makes it this far is entitled to a treat—a candy bar, handful of gumdrops, a chocolate chip cookie, an orange, or an apple. Children may not believe the river below could have carved out the gorge around them; this is a good place to talk about the power of water. Turn around if you have tired little hikers.

If you decide to go on, views get better as the trail re-enters forest. In another ½ mile, you emerge onto a promontory (elevation 1600 feet).

The trail continues on another mile, climbing through steep flower-covered meadows, past the site of the former Puppy Lookout (elevation 2520 feet), with views 30 miles up and down the river. The golden daisy lighting the way upward is called balsam root. This is far enough for any youngster. The Dog Mountain summit is 2940 feet.

63. Falls Creek Trail

Type: Dayhike
Difficulty: Moderate for children
Hikable: Year-round
One way: 1½ miles
High point: 1600 feet
Elevation gain: 300 feet
Green Trails map: No. 397 Wind River

A superb three-tiered waterfall lures the hiker at the end of a riverside trail. Listen. The sound of the creek from below the trail, beside it, and above it will cue your family to the nearness of the rapids and the waterfall. Have the kids listen carefully and guess how close they are to the cataract.

 Take I-5 to Vancouver, then State Highway 14 along Columbia River Road east to Carson. From Carson, drive the Wind River Road 14.5 miles to an intersection with the Mineral Springs Road, then continue north on the Wind River Road another 0.8 mile and turn right on Road No. 3062. Drive 2 miles and at the fork between the upper and lower falls trails, go right on Road No. (3062) 057 another 0.4 mile to the lower falls trailhead of Trail No. 152A (elevation 1300 feet).

Begin alongside the creek on a narrow winding trail, then watch the creek disappear into a ravine that deepens, then rises to trail level once more. Cross the creek at ¾ mile among huge old trees and begin

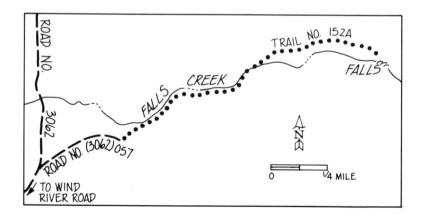

Falls Creek Falls

to climb up and away from the water. Point out to the kids that you must gain some elevation in order to reach the level of the waterfall. At 1¼ miles in spring and early summer pass under a trailside waterfall. Children love being splashed as they run under it, and some feel the waterfall is like a giant sprinkler.

Be prepared for all to stop in their tracks when they first see Falls Creek Falls. Only the upper two falls are visible through the trees at first, but the trail ends in ¼ mile more, directly in front of the plunge pool and lower falls. Aficionados of waterfalls rate this one with five stars. But Falls Creek is such a poor name for it. Maybe your children can think of a better name. Magnificent Falls would be more like it, don't you think?

64. Siouxon Creek

Type: Dayhike or overnight
Difficulty: Easy for children
Hikable: March–November
One way to West Creek Falls: 1½ miles
One way to Horseshoe Falls: 2 miles
High point: 1600 feet
Elevation loss and gain: 300 feet
Green Trails map: No. 396 Lookout Mountain
U.S. Forest Service map: Gifford Pinchot

This low-level river hike, accessible when snow buries higher trails, will appeal to children for several reasons. Close enough to the creek in a number of places to dip in toes and sample the current, the trail is relatively wide and level after an initial drop. The moss-covered forest alongside the trail has a magical Emerald City feel, with trilliums, ferns, and four-leaf-cloverlike oxalis. A number of waterfalls call out to be examined from above, beside, and below; one even has a possible campsite next to its plunge pool. This roadless forest, with its pockets of ancient trees, is rare natural regrowth from a historic 1902 fire which burned about 40,000 acres, the Yacolt Burn. Unfortunately, the regrown forest has been slated for harvest by the Forest Service under the principles of "New Forestry." Harvest is harvest, no matter what the euphemism. Once gone, such a roadless forest cannot be regained; you and your children may be the last generations to enjoy these trees. Siouxon Creek has been proposed for Wild and Scenic River status, which will preserve the river bottom but not the forested hillside.

 From I-5, take the Woodland exit east and drive 23.7 miles on State Highway 503 to Chelatchie, the headquarters of the Mount St. Helens National Volcanic Monument. (Be certain to make the obscure left turn near Yale or you will end up in Cougar.) At Chelatchie, go

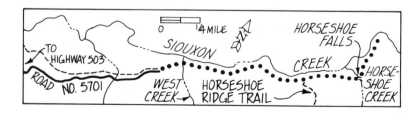

left on a county road that in 1.3 miles becomes Road No. 54. At 6.9 miles from Chelatchie, turn onto Road No. 57 and at 10.3 miles go left on Road No. 5701. The road ends 3.8 miles later at the unmarked trailhead No. 30 (elevation 1550 feet).

Find a trail to the left of the road, intersecting the Siouxon Creek Trail; go right and drop 300 feet to the valley floor. Kids don't mind going down, but save some energy treats for the return trip. The trail closely follows the creek's uphill bank; paths lead down to the creek and some nice pools. Old cedar stumps and logs abound on both sides—some have hollow cores. What kinds of animals make cozy

Siouxon Creek

homes in those hollow logs? Logs that have recently fallen across the trail have been cut away by trail builders, and their cut ends display their age. Explain to children that the rings that form in the tree represent each season's growth—fat rings for wet years, thin rings for dry years. The dark line allowing us to distinguish one ring from its neighbor is called latewood, formed at the very end of each growing season.

At ¼ mile you will hear and then see 40-foot West Creek Falls plunging beneath a small bridge and being channeled into a narrow funnel of gray-green rock. Children like crossing over the top of the waterfall and pausing midway to lean out and look down its face. Hang onto hands here. A safer vantage point is offered by a bench on the other side of the bridge, and an entirely different perspective can be reached by taking the ⅛-mile Falls Viewpoint path to the base of the falls. The trail ends at a possible single campsite or picnic area alongside the pool at the base of the fan-shaped falls. If you are tired, this is a possible turnaround point.

Follow the Siouxon upward. Rapids and white water increase as the trail leads on. Pass the trail to Horseshoe Ridge at 1 mile and watch for an overhanging cliff dappled with ferns and dripping, seeping moss. On a wet day every surface is saturated. Children love the squishing noises they can make as they pass by.

Regain lost elevation by returning to the main trail, stepping over several tiny creeklets. Siouxon Creek seems to gain in volume and turbulence, and children can look down on white-water rapids and fern-encrusted rock walls. At 2 miles come to another impressive waterfall viewpoint: Horseshoe Falls. Again benches have been provided for hikers who want to stop. Children can rest for a moment and ponder the enormous U-shaped bowl the river has created and the power of the waterfall. Far enough for a day. Pause and enjoy the beauty of the Siouxon.

65. Stairway to the Stars

Type: Dayhike
Difficulty: Difficult for children
Hikable: June–October
One way: 2½ miles
High point: 4390 feet
Elevation gain: 1500 feet
Green Trails maps: No. 396 Lookout Mountain,
No. 428 Bridal Veil
U.S. Forest Service map: Gifford Pinchot

The road to this trailhead is atrocious; the only justification for forcing the car upward is that you avoid having to walk it, and that once reached, the trail to the site of an old lookout on Silver Star Mountain is a delight. Parkland extends in every direction, with the white torches of beargrass dominant in May and June.

Children will want to know what happened to the forest that used to stand here. A few ancient gray snags hint at a long-ago disaster. The truth is that this is what remains of the famous Yacolt Burn of 1902, the largest and most destructive forest fire in state history. Two hundred thirty-eight thousand acres of forest were destroyed before rains finally contained the fire. "Why haven't the trees come back?" the kids ask. The soil still isn't ready for them, according to foresters who make studies of these beautiful meadows. But almost a century after the holocaust, kids can fly kites and run and play in the flowery meadows that are the legacy of the Yacolt Burn.

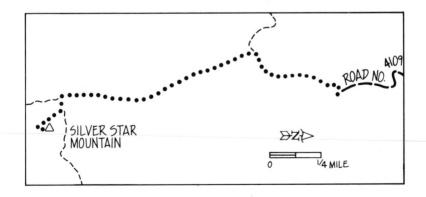

Mount Hood from Silver Star Mountain

The route described here is the abandoned lookout road, probably built in the 1930s. Finding trailheads in the maze of county, Department of Natural Resources, and Forest Service roads is a challenge, and some of the roads are in unbelievably bad condition. A Forest Service map is essential, and it would be wise to ask the Wind River ranger which road is best.

Drive State Highway 503 to Amboy and turn onto County Road No. 16 (which can also be reached through Battleground). Drive though the town of Yacolt, making first a left turn (unmarked), and in two blocks, at a stop sign, a right turn (also unmarked). At 3 miles from Yacolt, turn left on County Road No. 12, and in 7.5 miles reach the forest boundary and Sunset Campground. Turn right on Road No. 41, through the campground, cross the East Fork Lewis River, and start climbing. At 3.4 miles from the campground, make a nearly 360-degree turn onto Road No. 4109, and follow it 4 very rough miles to timberline, where it is blocked (elevation 3400 feet).

The hiking route follows the old service road, which is wide enough to let you hold a child's hand, and climbs upward in lush flower and grass fields to ever-expanding views of Mounts Adams, Rainier, and St. Helens, and out west beyond to forests and cities. In about 1¾ miles the road reaches a 4000-foot-high point. Children will want to begin looking ahead for the site of the old lookout and its stairway to nowhere, but they can't see it from here. The way then dips a bit into a forested saddle (ask them why they think trees can grow here), then climbs again. At 2¼ miles keep left at a junction and ascend more steeply on the badly eroded road to reach the summit ridge. Suddenly the lookout site appears and children can also see Mount Hood and the Columbia River too. The old lookout building is gone, but the three stairs leading up from what is left of the foundation make a great jumping-off place. Children can pretend they are waiting for liftoff, or getting ready to climb the stairway to the stars.

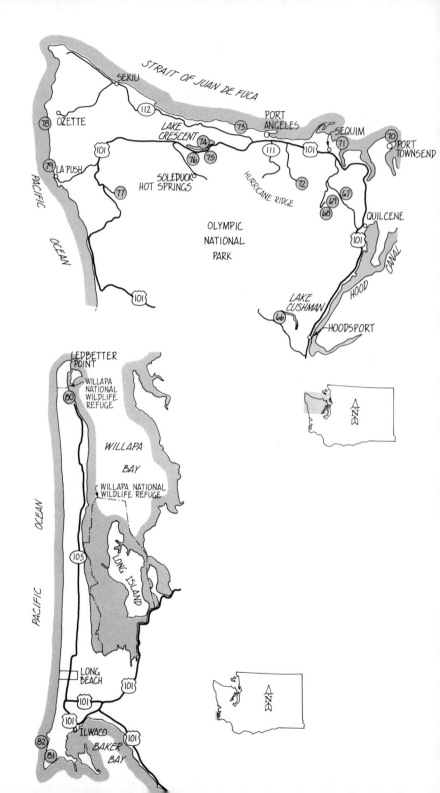

The Olympic Peninsula

66. South Fork Skokomish River

Type: Dayhike or overnight
Difficulty: Moderate for children
Hikable: April–November
One way to sandbar: 1¼ miles
One way to campsites: 6 miles
Elevation loss and gain: 400 feet
Green Trails map: No. 199 Mount Tebo
Custom Correct map: Mount Skokomish–Lake Cushman

Here is a short hike to a riverbank through old-growth forest with several attractions for children. In 1¼ mile they can reach a river with wide sand and gravel bars. On the way (if there is solitude) they can look for elk and deer; in the spring they may even see elk calves and deer fawns. Mother elk and deer shelter their babies in secret, nestlike hideaways. If you should approach a hidden fawn, the mother deer will act nonchalant, to fool you into thinking she has no fawn nearby. In contrast, a mother elk is likely to charge you to protect her calf. The best policy if you find a baby wild animal is to leave it alone. Most likely the mother is nearby.

The old trees have mossy green carpets beneath them, ornamented with ferns, trilliums, and three-lobed sweet-after-death. But the drop to the river level is steep, and the climb back up will be a pull for little children. Be prepared to encounter mountain bikers who love this trail, too. There are two trailheads—the first 2 miles of either are excellent for children. However, the farther one is 5 miles from the trailhead, gated from October to May to protect the elk, and was closed the day we were there, so only one is described here.

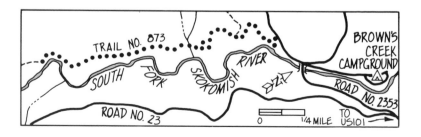

South Fork Skykomish River trail

From Shelton, drive north on U.S. Highway 101 for 6.5 miles, and turn upriver on the South Fork Skokomish River Recreation Area Road. In 5.7 miles go right on a road signed "BROWN'S CREEK CAMPGROUND." The road becomes Forest Road No. 23. Fifteen miles from U.S. Highway 101 reach a major junction. Straight ahead is the road that is gated in winter. Go right on Road No. 2353 towards Brown's Creek Campground, first crossing the South Fork Skokomish River, then go left, staying on Road No. 2353, and crossing Le Bar Creek. Go 0.5 mile to the trailhead (elevation 650 feet).

The South Fork Skokomish River Trail No. 873 begins on long switchbacks for ¼ mile, leading into luxuriant old-growth forest. Fallen cedar logs will raise questions in the minds of kids. How old were these trees? How long since they fell? Huge 300-year-old firs dominate the forest, but moss-wrapped roots rise from the ground like green octopus arms writhing beneath the sea. Big-leaf maple are also dressed in green velvet, and are studded with ferns up and down their branches and trunks. Children might feel they are in a special place and begin to whisper. If they don't, encourage them to whisper anyway. Elk and deer move through the forest silently and may appear unannounced if not alarmed by the sound of voices.

At ¼ mile look left down a steep bank to the South Fork. Here a trail taking off to the right leads away from the river and back to the logging road. Go straight ahead. Drop steeply on switchbacks for another ½ mile, passing over two creeks, to the river level.

At the bottom, step into an open glade with more mossy old maples. Parallel the river for another ¼ mile, then look for an off-trail route left to the riverbank. The Skokomish has often changed its channel, and where it has abandoned its course there remains a wide sandy bar. Children will enjoy the feeling of being on a beach, throwing sticks into the river and watching them be swept away. For children this is a great turnaround point.

The trail continues to follow the river, with more big trees and another sandbar, crosses the river at 6 miles on a log bridge to reach several campsites, then at about 7.5 miles climbs gently to the second trailhead on Road No. 2361, some 8 miles from the starting point.

67. Mount Zion

Type:	Dayhike
Difficulty:	Difficult for children
Hikable:	May–October
One way:	1¾ miles
High point:	4273 feet
Elevation gain:	1300 feet
Green Trails map:	No. 136 Tyler Peak
U.S. Forest Service map:	Olympic National Forest

This short but steep trail climbs 900 feet per mile through tree-size rhododendrons to a summit with a big view. Children will like the challenge of climbing a little mountain and they can be proud of the view they have earned: north to the Strait of Juan de Fuca, Mount Baker, and Discovery Bay; south to the skyscrapers of Seattle; and west to Port Townsend, the Dungeness Valley, and into the heart of the Olympic Mountains. The site of a former lookout, Mount Zion has a trail that varies from steep to very steep. This trail is open to

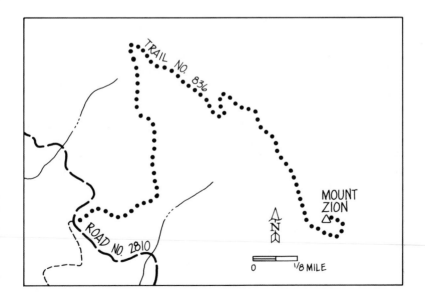

View from Mount Zion trail

motorcycles, but we have never encountered any or even seen their tracks. Plan your trip for mid-June, when walking through and under the pink native rhododendron blossoms reminds one of walking through a tropical forest.

From Quilcene, on Hood Canal, drive north on U.S. Highway 101 for 2 miles, and turn left on Lords Lake Road. Pass the Little Quilcene River Dam, after which the road becomes No. 28. Seven miles from U.S. Highway 101 keep right at an intersection with No. 27. At 8.5 miles reach Bon Jon Pass, turn right on Road No. 2810, and drive another 2 miles to the trailhead for the Mount Zion Trail No. 836 (elevation 2950 feet).

The trail starts up steeply, but the reward is a beautiful canopy of rhododendrons overhead, and an understory of ferns, twinflowers, Oregon grape, violets, and ocean spray. Because the trail is so steep, children can be coaxed with frequent energy stops and the promise of treats on top (elevation 4273 feet). Interesting rock formations suggesting marine origins provide seating for families who want to enjoy the views. Ask your children how rocks on the top of a mountain could once have been sandy tide flats under the ocean.

68. Dungeness River

Type: Dayhike or overnight
Difficulty: Moderate for children
Hikable: April–November
One way to Camp Handy: 3½ miles
High point: 3200 feet
Elevation gain: 700 feet
Custom Correct map: Buckhorn Wilderness
Green Trails map: No. 136 Tyler Peak

Children should experience this beautiful river valley, with its awe-inspiring enormous old trees next to white water rapids. The Dungeness River has been proposed for Wild and Scenic River status. The easy and fairly level trail follows the Dungeness for many miles in both unprotected national forest and the Buckhorn Wilderness. The trail also offers an interesting contrast in climates: the first 2½ miles are in lush rain forest; then the trail climbs into the rain shadow of the Olympics, and the environment becomes as dry as an eastern Washington forest. The ultimate reward is in seeing the meadows high above the Dungeness River.

Drive U.S. Highway 101 toward Port Angeles, to 0.1 mile south of the entrance to Sequim Bay State Park and turn left on Louella Road. At 0.9 mile go left and follow the Palo Alto Road, which eventually becomes Forest Service Road No. 28. At 7.4 miles from U.S. 101, keep right onto Forest Road No. 2860. Pass East Crossing Campground, cross the Dungeness River, and start climbing. At 12.3 miles is a switchback and intersection with Road No. 2870; stay left on 2860. At 17.2 miles the road dips down to reach the Upper Dungeness Trail No. 833 at 18.8 miles (elevation 2500 feet).

Begin up two short switchbacks to a level shelf alongside the river. In early spring the trail can be muddy. I met three little boys with

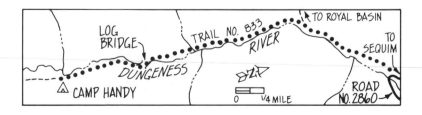

muddy tennis shoes, who were clearly enjoying stamping their feet into the mire at every step. Wind up and down through moss-lined cedar stumps, with woodland plants such as oak fern, vanilla leaf, sweet-after-death, occasional rhododendrons, and yew trees. At 1 mile find an excellent riverside camp at the confluence of the Dungeness and Royal Creek. The camps next to the bridge would make a fine turnaround or picnic site, or a base camp if a family wants to carry overnight gear only this far before walking on to Camp Handy. The Royal Basin Trail also departs from this junction.

Camp Handy Shelter on Dungeness River trail

The trail continues through beautiful ancient trees alongside the river. Fishermen love to cast from mossy boulders and logs along the way. At 2 miles children should look for a salt lick frequently used by deer, porcupines, and other animals. If you are lucky you will see deer there. If not, your children will have to be contented with examining the assortment of animal tracks around it. Cross Royal Creek on a log at 2½ miles, and climb a hillside. Look out to the beginning of the first alpine meadows, dry because they are in the rain shadow of the range. Children can look for shrubs such as Rocky Mountain juniper. At 3 miles cross the Dungeness River on a sturdy log. The water looks threatening, and the handrail is too high for a little child, so be ready to help.

Camp Handy, at 3½ miles, is a three-sided shelter so popular that a family should not count on being able to stay inside it. But the open meadow contains a campsite by the river and one more lies in the grove south of the shelter. Enjoy the view over the meadows of the Upper Dungeness Valley. This area was never covered by the continental ice-age glaciers, and was isolated for thousands of years, so some of its plants are unique or rare. Even the marmots are different. Some plants have close relatives many hundreds of miles away. Kids can imagine this meadow long ago as an island rising above the ice fields.

69. Tubal Cain Mine

Type:	Dayhike or overnight
Difficulty:	Difficult for children
Hikable:	May–November
One way:	3¾ miles
High point:	4300 feet
Elevation gain:	1000 feet
Custom Correct map:	Buckhorn Wilderness
Green Trails map:	No. 136 Tyler Peak

A historic mining area dating from the turn of the century offers children a chance to walk into an old tunnel that still smells of sulfur, and to explore mining relics at what is left of the mining camp. Older children will want to find the broken sluice box and two-inch iron pipe beside a ruined shaft ventilator, and to search for the Pelton wheels and the old power plant below camp.

Tell them Tubal Cain was the Biblical smith who forged bronze and iron tools—a fitting name for the mine, since iron and copper were being sought here. Thirty years before the mining claim, an exploring party must have met a bear here, because early hikers found a tiny grave with cross dated August 5, 1865, beside an old tree, paying tribute to a dog killed by a bear in the explorers' defense. This trail is a rhododendron garden of unsurpassed beauty from mid- to late June.

Drive U.S. Highway 101 toward Port Angeles, to 0.1 mile south of the entrance to Sequim Bay Park, and turn left on Louella Road. At 0.9 mile go left and follow Palo Alto Road, which eventually becomes Forest Service Road No. 28, a gravel road with mountain views and some scary exposures. At 7.4 miles from U.S. 101, keep right on Forest

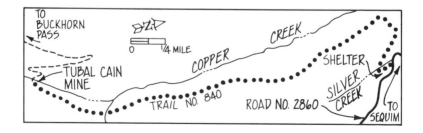

Tubal Cain Mine artifacts

Road No. 2860. Pass East Crossing, cross the Dungeness River (Hike 68), and start climbing. At 12.3 miles is a switchback and an intersection with Road No. 2870; keep left on Road No. 2860. At 17.2 miles the road dips downward; at 18.8 miles recross the Dungeness River, pass through a gate (closed in winter), and at 22.7 miles reach the trailhead for Tubal Cain Mine Trail No. 840 (elevation 3300 feet).

Begin the trail alongside Silver Creek and a three-sided shelter, where one could get out of the weather if necessary. Cross the creek and begin a gradual ascent through a garden of rhododendrons, moss, and forest flowers. Enter the Buckhorn Wilderness at ¼ mile and look up the valley for the snow and rocks of Mount Buckhorn through the trees.

Along the way, steep creeks cascade directly down the mountain beside the trail, over it, and straight down below. None is too wide to step over, and children will enjoy walking over these waterfalls. Picture pack trains of mules burdened with dynamite on the same trail. At 3 miles is a small mine tunnel just above the trail. As a mining venture, Tubal Cain was a failure. Not a penny's profit was ever recorded, despite an estimated $200,000 investment over a twenty-five-year period.

Reach the old townsite at 3¼ miles. Cross Copper Creek at 3¾ miles and look left, at the base of Iron Mountain, for a 100-foot slope of mine tailings. Tubal Cain's drilling took the miners 2800 feet into the mountain, with 1500 feet of side tunnels. Climb the soft dirt trail to the rock tunnel, and be prepared for a whiff of old sulfur. Families with boots and flashlights will want to at least step inside, but go no farther. In 1972 the shaft was still passable for 600 feet, but no mine tunnel can ever be considered safe, so don't go far. The water running underfoot may come from melting snow or from springs deep inside Iron Mountain.

Explore either or both of the two living areas. Copper City is another 500 feet up the trail toward Marmot Pass, while Tull City is below the tunnel. These "cities" were inaccessible for much of the year. Because electricity was not available here in 1904, a log dam (long gone) provided water power generation for the drills and sawmill needed to build a bunkhouse for thirty-five men, a cookhouse, an office, a powder house, and a blacksmith shop. (In the winter of 1912, avalanches wrecked some of the buildings the men were staying in.) Children can look for bits of rusty iron and broken glass to suggest the locations of the bunkhouse and cookhouse. A lot of dreams and hard work were invested in this place: listen for echoes of the ghosts that haunt Tubal Cain.

70. Point Wilson

Type: Dayhike
Difficulty: Easy for children
Hikable: Year-round
One way: 1¼ mile
Elevation gain: None
Map: Jefferson County road map

A fine sandy beach extends beneath high bluffs and between two access points on the way to the Point Wilson lighthouse. The hike can be made in either direction: children won't care. Of all the hikes along the strait, this may be the one children will love the best. Water and sand play possibilities are infinite. On a clear day, Mount Baker stands as guardian over them as they wade, dig, build sand castles, and throw sticks to dogs to fetch from out in the waves.

Cars may be left at either end of the walk. To begin at the west end, drive to Port Townsend and find the city courthouse. From there, follow signs to Fort Worden State Park. At the entrance, turn left on W Street, angle right on Spruce, left on Admiralty, curve right on San Juan Avenue, then left on 49th, and right on Kuhn Street to the road end at the North Beach of Fort Worden State Park. A trailless lagoon along the way is called Chinese Gardens because at one time Chinese immigrants grew truck-farm produce around it.

Begin walking east beside low banks covered with beach grass. Children can watch for giant oil tankers and container cargo ships passing close enough to make waves lap the beach beside them. Take binoculars and look at the ships' flags. Ask kids to figure out which countries the ships come from. At low tide the wide, sandy shore is easy walking and offers kids the chance to write their names or leave messages in the sand. The bank quickly becomes high, sandy cliff, sloughing off with winter rains to add to the beach sand. Children

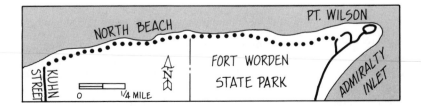

Point Wilson from North Beach

may be surprised to see long-necked, black cormorants perched on rocks in deeper water, with wings outspread to dry their feathers. Without warning they will dive deep to find a fish. The rocks are covered with sharp-edged barnacles, interesting for kids to inspect closely. Each acorn barnacle looks like a miniature empty gray volcano, which comes alive when the tide covers it. The animal extends its featherlike legs to catch microscopic food drifting by.

Children should imagine this place in May 1792 when Captain George Vancouver and a party of men, anchored in Discovery Bay, started out to explore the coastline. The fog was heavy when Vancouver pushed around this small headland, which he named Point Wilson for a friend, so he was not aware of the size of this body of water until the sun broke through the fog. Vancouver was so impressed with the beauty of this setting and the extent and character of the bay that he named it Port Townsend for a famous English marquis of the time. Kids may think it strange that these places were named for men who never saw them.

Views are wonderful across to Vancouver Island, the San Juans, the high bluffs of Whidbey Island, and the snow-covered Cascades beyond them. Round a small cove and continue the walk to the red-roofed Coast Guard lighthouse at Point Wilson, built in 1913. Unfortunately, the building is off-limits to visitors now, but there are picnic tables nearby, recessed out of the wind, should you want to stop for lunch. A functioning radar tower and the wreck of an old surveillance tower are standing nearby. Cars can be left at either end of the walk.

Point Wilson Lighthouse

71. Gibson Spit

Type: Dayhike
Difficulty: Easy for children
Hikable: Year-round
One way: 1 mile
High point: Sea level
Elevation gain: None
U.S. Forest Service map: Olympic National Forest

Walk with children at any time of the year in any weather along a low spit curving out across Sequim Bay. Children can expect to see mud-probing shorebirds on the bay side and gulls swooping on the strait side, along with an occasional otter playing in the surf right next to the beach. In May and June, pigeon guillemots nest on tiny perches high on the cliffs above. Once in a while a loon, with its distinctive black and white stripes, visits the bay. The view sweeps out to the Strait of Juan de Fuca and the tip of Dungeness Spit, and back to warmer Sequim Bay, wrapped on one side by Travis Spit and on the

Shells found on Gibson Spit

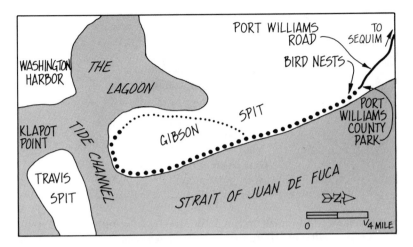

other by Gibson Spit. This hike has the attraction of a tidal surge so strong the current ripples like a river.

Drive U.S. Highway 101 north to Sequim. At the first stoplight, turn right on Sequim Avenue, which becomes Sequim–Dungeness Road. At 1 mile turn right on Port Williams Road and at 2.4 miles reach the road's end and park at the Marlyn Nelson County Park at Port Williams. This is the only public access, as the Battelle Institute owns the land east of the spit.

As hikers begin this walk, the two spits appear to blend into one. Children might think they can walk all the way to the opposite shore of Sequim Bay, but as they continue they will find the way blocked by a narrow opening of swift water.

From the parking lot, as you go under the cliffs to the right, look up for the nesting birds. Gibson Spit pulls away from the bank, and reaches out across Sequim Bay. Open water appears between Gibson and Travis spits, and children can see the tips of both spits. When the tide is rushing in or out, the current is as swift as any river. Families can see the action of the tides and can talk about what causes them, and how their effects may have formed the two spits and the lagoon.

Eventually the way is blocked by a passage into the "lagoon." Turn around and on the way back explore the lagoon, the little bay behind the spit. The mud flats of the lagoon are a salt marsh that nurtures many tiny marine creatures. These, in turn, attract all manner of sandpipers, gulls, and herons. Children can clearly see their tracks. Listen for the high squeaking "*keeep*" note of the sandpipers. Some of these birds prefer mud to sand because their favorite foods live in mud. Children can understand preferring mud to just about anything else.

72. Blue Mountain

Type: Dayhike
Difficulty: Easy for children
Hikable: July–October
One way: ¼ mile
High point: 6007 feet
Elevation gain: 250 feet
Green Trails map: No. 135 Port Angeles

An easy ¼-mile walk on an abandoned road seems to lead to the top of the world. Young children will enjoy the challenge of reaching the site of a fire lookout built in 1931 on the top of the mountain, where the family will find a breathtaking view of the Olympic Mountains and the waterways of the Strait of Juan de Fuca, Victoria, Vancouver Island, Bellingham, and Mount Baker. Children will be intrigued with the tiny oceangoing ships, like toy boats in a bathtub, and the plume of smoke rising from a pulp mill in distant Port Angeles, and by a solar-powered radio structure near the top of Blue Mountain.

From Sequim, drive west on U.S. Highway 101 some 11 miles. About 4 miles short of downtown Port Angeles, near milepost 253, turn south and go uphill 17 miles on the Deer Park Road. The first 5 miles are paved; beyond, the road becomes progressively steeper and more narrow. At 16 miles pass the Deer Park Campground and continue upward another mile to the road end (elevation 5750 feet).

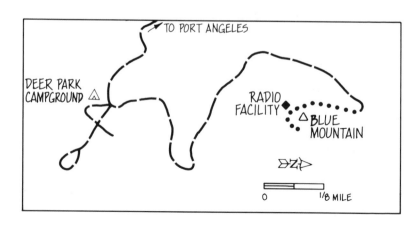

Hike the abandoned road upward in subalpine forest and meadows as it traverses the west side of the mountain. Children can walk holding hands with parents on the wide old roadbed to reach the broad summit that once housed a lookout (elevation 6007 feet). The lookout was removed in the 1950s, but children can imagine what it might have been like to spend a heroic summer up here, spotting and telegraphing the location of the first wisp of smoke, before it could grow into a dangerous forest fire. Expect them to be overwhelmed with the vastness and the beauty of the Olympic Mountains.

Elk Mountain from Blue Mountain trail

73. Freshwater Bay

Type: Dayhike
Difficulty: Moderate for children
Hikable: Year-round
One way: 2½ miles
Elevation gain: None
Map: Olympic National Forest/Olympic National Park

Walk a rocky beach cove along the Strait of Juan de Fuca on Freshwater Bay; the scenery is varied and interesting. If the kids watch the horizon for marine traffic, they will see an assortment of powerboats, sailboats, occasional kayaks, barges, freighters, and container cargo ships, headed for Port Angeles and Puget Sound. Children who are fortunate or very observant may even spot marine traffic of the natural variety: whales and seals. They might also encounter scuba divers, who collect Pacific abalone and kelp greenling from deep below the surface, and Indians and local folks who collect clams, crab, and oysters at low tides. Kids can watch and enjoy the sea harvest, or simply throw rocks and wade into the gentle waves of this protected cove. But children should take no marine life and disturb nothing they see.

Plan on taking at least half a day to walk to a turnaround point at Covall Creek. At high tide there is no beach, so check the tide table before starting out, and make sure you turn around before the tide

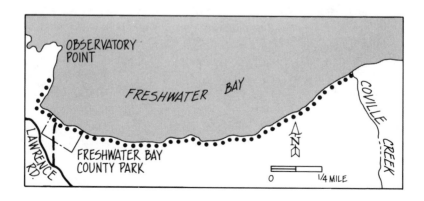

Boat launch at Freshwater Bay

comes back in. Children will need sturdy boots to walk through wet sand and rocks.

From Port Angeles drive U.S. Highway 101 west 4.6 miles and go right on Road No. 112, signed "JOYCE." Follow Road No. 112 another 4.2 miles and turn right on Gerber Road. Go 2.5 miles more to Lawrence Road and follow it west to Freshwater Bay County Park, where the road ends and there is a boat launch.

Look west to Observatory Point where there was a World War II installation. Walk east (right) under a tall bank. The marine life along the way—the crabs, seals, fish, birds, and kelp beds—are remnants of the beach life once relied upon by Native cultures everywhere, and visible in only a few places today.

74. Spruce Railroad

Type:	Dayhike
Difficulty:	Moderate for children
Hikable:	Year-round
One way to first tunnel:	1 mile
One way to second tunnel:	3¼ miles
One way with shuttle:	4½ miles
High point:	650 feet
Elevation gain:	50 feet
Custom Correct map:	Lake Crescent–Happy Lake Ridge
Green Trails map:	No. 101 Lake Crescent

This historic railroad grade with ruined tunnels offers children a level lakeshore walk, a swim, a chance to examine the entrances to two tunnels, and the opportunity to look down from a bridge into the Devil's Punchbowl. On a hot day whole families have been known to jump into chilly Lake Crescent to cool off. Parents should tell kids that the Spruce Railroad was built by the U.S. Government to carry out spruce for World War I airplane wings. The war ended before any spruce was carried, but the tracks did carry carloads of logs and workers on the Port Angeles Western Railroad along the lake's north shore until the 1950s. Old-timers tell of crossties made of alder and maple, which quickly rotted (explaining the nickname "The P. A. Wobbly"), and of the sunken locomotive resting in one of the coves. Another legend has it that train employees ate fruit as they traveled, and that

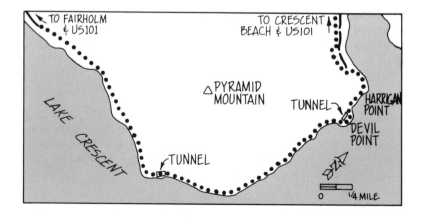

Spruce Railroad Trail over Devil's Punchbowl

where they tossed apple cores and cherry pits out the windows, fruit trees stand today.

Drive west from Port Angeles on U.S. Highway 101. Between Lake Sutherland and Lake Crescent, near milepost 232, turn right at East Beach Road, signed "CRESCENT BEACH–PIEDMONT." At 3.3 miles go left, crossing the Lyre River at the outlet of the lake. At 4 miles reach the trailhead parking lot and walk 200 feet to the trailhead. The apple trees here are remnants from the orchard of an old homestead.

For a 4½ mile, one-way hike, leave one car here and go back to U.S. Highway 101. Drive around the lake to Fairholm at the west end. Turn right on a road signed "Campground–Camp David Junior." Pass the campground, at 1.5 miles pass Camp David Junior, and at 5 miles reach the road end and the Spruce Railroad Trail.

For a round trip with children, I recommend beginning at the eastern end of the trail. Start on a wide, muddy path with a sign warning of poison oak ahead. Don't expect to see it until the rocky cliff section of the trail, but prepare children not to touch any low-growing plants. At ½ mile drop 50 feet to the lakeshore. Powerboats zoom close to the bank, creating wake that laps beside you. The lapping sound is delightful to hear on a hot day. At about ¾ mile, there is a small meadow with a picnic area, and the best place for beginners to swim.

Just before 1 mile, children should look for the first collapsed railroad tunnel, to the right of the trail. They will be excited about exploring it, but tell them that the tunnel is extremely unsafe to enter now. Contour around the ridge the tunnel penetrated, and gaze down at the Devil's Punchbowl, a small, deep-blue cove crossed by an arching bridge. Many families never get beyond this magical point. Ask children to imagine that if the lake were drained, this trail would be high on the edge of a cliff. Fishermen love to cast for the lake's unique trout, the Beardsley, from this bridge. Beyond here the trail has some patches of poison oak. Around the corner, the other side of the tunnel can be inspected by climbing a short way above the trail.

If your family has the energy to continue, the trail stretches along a cliffside ledge to a second tunnel at 3¼ miles. Take a flashlight to the mouth. This tunnel may be inspected more closely than the first one, although fallen rocks and collapsed beams cover the floor. Now have the children turn and look across the deep-blue lake to the Lake Crescent Lodge, then up to Storm King Mountain. If you were on a Scottish loch in the Highlands, the scene would look very much like this. The trail continues the length of the lake.

75. Marymere Falls

Type: Dayhike
Difficulty: Easy for children
Hikable: Year-round
One way: 1¼ miles
High point: 1000 feet
Elevation gain: 400 feet
Custom Correct map: Lake Crescent–Happy Lake Ridge
Green Trails map: No. 101 Lake Crescent

Much like movies and restaurants, waterfalls can be evaluated and rated with stars for their scenic qualities. This four-star waterfall with a short and easy access trail has been a favorite with families for generations. The trail, through old-growth forest, is wide and level for ¾ mile before crossing Barnes Creek and starting up the ridge alongside the falls. Children love walking its log bridge and climbing up alongside the waterfall. They run ahead to scout what comes next, then run back to report to parents.

Drive U.S. Highway 101 to Lake Crescent, 21.5 miles west of Port
Angeles. Turn right on the road signed "Lake Crescent Lodge–Marymere

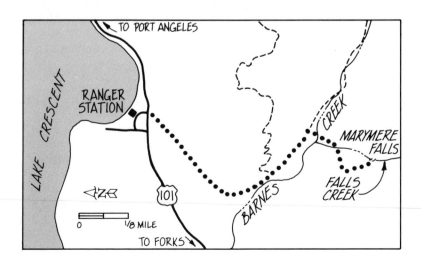

Marymere Falls

FALLS." In a few feet go right again to a large parking lot (elevation 600 feet).

Start on a level trail that passes the old ranger station, then crosses under U.S. Highway 101. Kids will enjoy running through the underpass beside the creek and listening to the echoes of vehicles overhead. The trail parallels the highway for a long ¼ mile, then turns inland beside Barnes Creek. A junction with the Storm King Mountain Trail is marked with an enormous boulder at ¾ mile. (Don't take children up that trail—it's steep!) Continue through vine maples reaching for the sun, beneath ancient cedars. The log bridge with railings across Barnes Creek has only one lane, so this busy trail sometimes has lines of people waiting to cross the bridge, but the setting is so beautiful that not even children become impatient. (Some kids love stepping out over the water and being the center of attention for all those waiting their turn.)

Another log bridge over Falls Creek is the preamble to the climb up the falls. The trail has railings and ninety-one wooden steps for the safety of old and very young hikers. There is even a loop, with one trail section for the upward bound and another for the downward bound. (Go right and don't fight the crowd—the downward flow is overwhelming.)

A bench opposite the 98-foot falls allows a close-up view of the catch basin and a breath of spray. Kids will sit transfixed watching the water drop. Take a camera to try to capture the tiered column of water framed by moss-covered cliffs and maidenhair fern. Enough to stand here and gaze at beautiful Marymere, then have the children pose for pictures in front of it.

76. North Fork Soleduck River

Type:	Dayhike or overnight
Difficulty:	Moderate for children
Hikable:	April–November
One way to meadow:	1¼ miles
High point:	1800 feet
Elevation gain and loss:	300 feet
Custom Correct map:	Lake Crescent–Happy Lake Ridge

This lightly used woodland trail follows the north fork of the Soleduck into a meadow that can be either a base camp for further explorations up the river, or a turnaround point. In August and September children can expect to see spawning salmon from the bridge or from natural rock benches along the riverbank. Elk and deer are frequent visitors all year round, and if children miss seeing them they may find their tracks instead. The elk act as lawnmowers and grounds-keepers for the forest, grooming and trimming plants such as devil's club and salmonberries so that the trail looks neat and tidy. A family's best chance to see the big animals is in the fall and winter months, either early in the morning or late in the evening. This river has been proposed for Wild and Scenic River designation.

 From Port Angeles drive 30 miles west on U.S. Highway 101 to the Soleduck Hot Springs Road. Turn right and at 8.3 miles look for the trailhead on the left side of the road (elevation 1500 feet).

Begin by climbing up and over a 300-foot ridge separating the two forks of the river. If children huff and puff, tell them that in ½ mile it will be all downhill. (Don't mention the return.) As the sounds of the Soleduck die away, the trail levels out and begins to drop. Old

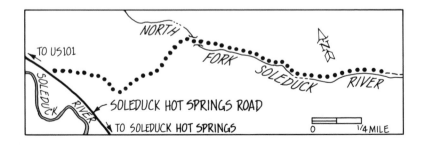

cedar stumps and prone nurse logs are part of a fairyland of moss, oak fern, and twinflowers. One giant log has a 5-foot cut facing the trail. Have the kids count as many of the rings as they can to get a sense of its age. Or stand them against the log to get another kind of feel for its size. Children can watch for spotted "appaloosa" (spotted like the horses) slugs (actually banana slugs) chewing their way along through forest greenery.

At 1 mile look down on the North Fork Soleduck. At 1¼ miles cross it on a log bridge, and hang on to children if they aren't tall enough to reach the railing. In late summer this is a great place to watch spawning salmon swimming upstream. Tell children that spawning females actually dig a small nest, or redd, with their tails in which to lay their eggs. The narrow elk-groomed glade begins on the other side of the bridge, the turnaround.

For those who choose to continue, many good campsites present themselves for another ½ mile. Narrow river chutes where the water is channeled through a funnel occur at 2⅓ and 2½ miles, with wonderful expanses of bedrock right at river level, where children can also watch for fish or at least admire the white-water rapids. The river trail extends for 9 miles; you might choose to camp and continue your explorations.

North Fork Soleduck River trail

77. Bogachiel River

Type: Dayhike or overnight
Difficulty: Moderate for children
Hikable: June–November
One way to Bogachiel River: 2 miles
One way to Mosquito Creek: 3 miles
High point: 400 feet
Elevation gain: None
Custom Correct map: Bogachiel Valley
Green Trails map: No. 101 Lake Crescent

An elk-groomed rain-forest river valley offers families all of the primitive magic of the Hoh area, without the crowds. Huge, moss-shrouded second-growth maples and alders lean over the trail, then give way to even more beautiful old-growth forest pruned by resident herds of elk. As the elk lose more habitat to logging, they clip ever more diligently any wayward buttercup, salmonberry, sword fern, thimbleberry, or devil's club. The groomed, parklike result would make a British garden club gasp. There will be more elk tracks on the trail than people tracks. Have kids guess the size of the animals from the tracks. Follow the almost level trail to the river at 2 miles and to Mosquito Creek at 3 miles.

Drive west 1.1 miles on U.S. Highway 101 from Port Angeles, passing through the town of Forks, to Bogachiel State Park. Turn left on Undi Road and drive 4 miles to the trailhead. Park at a gate on the old road into the park (elevation 400 feet).

At present the trail drops onto private property and an abandoned roadbed. The first 2 miles may eventually be reconstructed on Forest Service land away from the river. For now, begin on private property on another old roadbed marked for possible logging or a subdivision. At 1 mile look across Kahkwa Creek to the right to see the remnants of early-day homesteads—old pastures and the ruins of barns and fences. Along the way have kids look for wedge-shaped fungus called conks, growing on the trunks of spruce, fir, and hemlock. They are a sign of the health and diversity of the rain forest. Children may also see bright orange chicken-of-the woods mushrooms growing like coral on tree trunks along the trail.

Enter the park at 1½ miles in woodland meadow lighted with filtered sunlight and hear the screeing sound of chickarees (Douglas squirrels) warning of your approach. Children can watch for elk all

Bogachiel rain forest

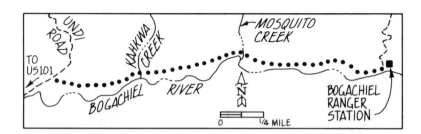

the way, but don't expect to hear them move. Despite their 1000-pound bulk, elk can move through brush almost silently. Children may want to know that elk feed in upland flats by day, then move slowly back down by night on established paths to the river to bed down on grassy river bars.

Continue on through old cedar stumps, cut early in the century, into second-growth hemlock forest, and reach the Bogachiel River at about 2 miles. A good camp here would make a possible turnaround point.

Grassy meadows between you and the river are also elk-cropped, and represent old flood plains, called benches, of the Bogachiel. The rain forest becomes increasingly wild and luxuriant as you move upriver.

Climb a few feet for the first time, and from a bench viewpoint look down on the wide riverbed, draining Bogachiel and Misery peaks. You can see some distance up and down the meandering channel and wide flood plain. At Mosquito Creek, at 3 miles, choose from grass-covered gravel bars for a campsite. If your children are willing, you might leave gear here and continue on another 2½ miles to the old Bogachiel ranger station and horse-barn shelter. But beware! The farther you go the greater are your chances of falling under the enchantment of the Bogachiel.

78. Sand Point

Type:	Dayhike or overnight
Difficulty:	Moderate for children
Hikable:	Year-round
One way to Sand Point:	3 miles
One way to Wedding Rock:	4½ miles
High point:	120 feet
Elevation gain:	120 feet
Custom Correct map:	Ozette Beach Loop
Green Trails map:	No. 1305 Ozette

Two trails depart from the Lake Ozette Campground. The preferred trail is Sand Point, which is shorter than the one to Cape Alava, and easier because it is *all* on boardwalk. The sandy beach is more attractive to kids than the cannonball-shaped rocks at Cape Alava. Possible campsites are protected from the wind by trees that shelter, shade, and frame beach views. If you wish, you can camp at Sand Point, continue up the beach past Indian petroglyphs to Cape Alava, camp again, and return to the trailhead, but Sand Point alone is a fine beach destination.

Drive west from Port Angeles on U.S. Highway 101; in 4.6 miles turn right on Road No. 112, which takes you along the Strait of Juan de Fuca past Sekiu. Turn left on the Ozette Lake Road and drive 21 miles to the ranger station, campground, and parking lot (elevation 36 feet).

Begin by crossing Ozette Creek on an arching concrete bridge. In 100 yards the trail forks; take the left fork to Sand Point. Children will delight in climbing up onto the springy boardwalk, sometimes almost 2 feet above the forest floor. They feel they are "following the yellow brick road" to the ocean. The dense, lush underbrush, the result of almost constant precipitation nine months of the year, has a magical quality when surveyed from a board sidewalk. Evergreen huckleberry, salal, young cedars, and hemlocks tangle together on either side. Several huge old-growth cedars occur together at about 1 mile, having escaped the fires that took out their neighbors. Immense upended fir root wads face the trail in several places. Kids will want to stop and examine the underside of a tree trunk. There is no taproot. "Whatever held it in place?" they may ask. It makes one wonder how such giants remain upright.

After 3 miles the trail descends to a campsite and a short way

Wedding Rock near Sand Point

farther to wide sandy beaches, scenic sea stacks, and inaccessible rock islands receding in the distance. We saw an eagle and a pair of raccoons. Children should be warned against trying to feed the raccoons, which have become so tame they beg from hikers and tear open packsacks. Be careful: raccoons will bite the hand that feeds them.

Rangers tell us the bears can be a problem, and campers will need to hang their food from a tree. When my children and I went backpacking at Sand Point many years ago we had a bear experience. We walked out to the ocean intending to hike for a week. We had a lovely sunset and slept well in a tent and driftwood shelter. The next morning Mama Bear and her cub smelled my homemade maple syrup

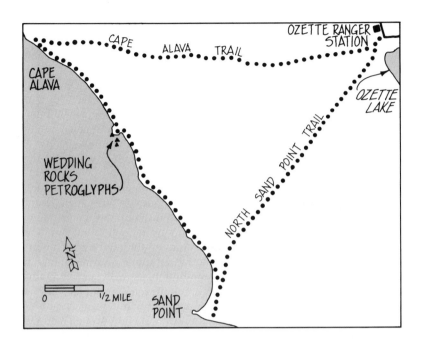

and came close for a helping. We threw rocks and banged on pots and pans, but she was undeterred. In fact, she was getting cross about our lack of hospitality. What could we do? She had us with our backs to the sea. Finally, we retreated and that was the end of our beach hike. It made an exciting and funny story for the kids to tell their friends for years, but I wished we had gone north the extra 1½ miles on the beach to see the Indian petroglyphs. The petroglyphs (maybe just early graffiti) are located at the high-tide mark on the only rock outcropping. Look carefully, because you can easily walk past them.

79. Hole in the Wall

Type:	Dayhike or overnight
Difficulty:	Easy when tide is out, difficult when tide is in
Hikable:	Year-round
One way:	1¼ miles
Elevation gain:	None
Custom Correct map:	North Olympic Coast
Green Trails map:	No. 130S Ozette

The power and majesty of the ocean waves here will awe kids. These waves are not to be trifled with. They throw enormous stumps and logs far up the beach and reduce headlands to gravel and sand. Explain to children how the block-shaped rock 2 miles out to sea, Cake Rock, was once attached to the mainland, but wave action has made it an island. The walk down the beach to Hole in the Wall, also carved by wave action, is a thrilling adventure for children. The Ellen Creek crossing at 1 mile can be somewhat difficult and hazardous if tides are high. Be prepared: carry a current tide table. Hiking above the high-tide mark is possible but more difficult than when the tide is low.

 Drive west approximately 50 miles from Port Angeles on U.S. Highway 101 and just 2 miles north of Forks turn right on the La Push–Mora road. Pass the Mora Campground and drive to the end of the road at the Rialto Beach parking lot (elevation 10 feet).

Start by walking right (north) along a few forested yards of trail, then cross driftwood to reach the sloping shoreline. Children are fascinated by the surf. When a skidding wave puts on its brakes, it kicks up pebbles and rocks in its path, then recedes in tongues of

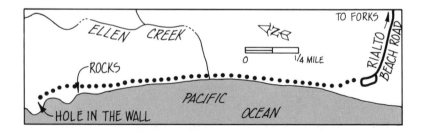

Hole in the Wall

foam like a bubble bath with a clatter as it drags the same pebbles back down the beach. Kids may find the walking slow going in the sand and rocks if the tide is high, but will be rewarded by the beach-combing possibilities. Have them look for polished pebbles of white quartz or scraps of wood shaped like animals or ray guns. They may wish to play in the piles of spent foam called spindrift.

Cross Ellen Creek at 1 mile on a combination of logs and stumps. The brown water is stained harmlessly by cedar roots and can be treated with iodine or filtered for drinking. There are campsites here for families interested in backpacking to the first ocean beach camp. This is also a possible turnaround point if you don't care to cross the creek.

Hole in the Wall is guarded by three sentinels. Sea stacks once connected to the mainland have been carved and isolated as mono-lithic rocks. Around the cove beyond the last one, children can see sky through the hole in Hole in the Wall. If the tide is low, they may even walk through it. To continue up the beach, when the tide is in, climb up the steep trail over the headland. However, you may want to linger in this cove and enjoy the superb beachcombing and tide pools containing starfish, swaying seaweeds, and anemones.

Offshore rocks from Hole in the Wall

80. Leadbetter Point

Type:	Dayhike
Difficulty:	Moderate for children
Hikable:	Year-round
One way on beach walk:	1¼ miles
Forest loop:	2¼ miles
High point:	10 feet
Elevation gain:	None
Map:	Washington State road map

Blue herons and geese winter here, in the spring hundreds of thousands of shorebirds migrate through with a great rushing of wings, and in the summer endangered snowy plovers nest, protected, in the National Wildlife Refuge. Although you can hear the surf, the ocean beach is inaccessible from here, but you can follow state park trails leading across Willapa Bay mud flats, pine forest, bogs, and sand dunes—all with their diverse plant and animal species. Because part of the point is a National Wildlife Refuge, children will find tracks of deer, elk, cottontail rabbits, raccoons, and shorebirds in the wet sand. At low tide one can walk for miles on the sandy beach of Willapa Bay, exploring the vegetation-covered sand dunes. Salt-tolerant eelgrass and glasswort on the bay side seem to attract deer and elk, judging from tracks and munched plants. Could these plants taste like pickles to them?

Drive to the Long Beach Peninsula. In the town of Seaview, leave

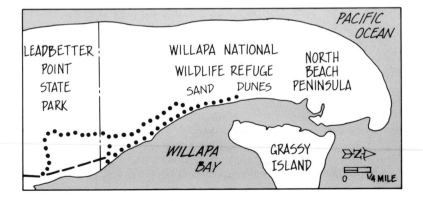

Black brants

U.S. Highway 101 and drive north 11 miles to Ocean Park and a choice: either go right and follow the road past Oysterville to Stackpole Road, or go straight ahead following the lefts and rights to Stackpole Road. Either way is about 6 miles. Follow Stackpole Road north a final 4.5 miles to the road end and a parking lot at Leadbetter Point State Park (elevation 20 feet). Camping is not allowed.

From the parking lot choose one of three directions to go: right leads directly to Willapa Bay, left leads to the forest loop described later, and straight ahead are miles of tree-covered sand dunes. For children, our suggestion is to walk north through the sand dunes looking for animal tracks. Once we actually saw a small bear on this walk, which later, as the children repeated the story, grew so large that it must have been a grizzly. Return to the starting point by the beach.

Beach walk: For this route go left a short ¼ mile, then make your way northward ½ mile on a maze of unmarked trails. Watch for coyote droppings and tracks. The best place for tracks is on the inland trails that go north through the old dunes. Cottontail rabbits land on their hind legs with the two front ones together almost as one, so kids can look for their telltale three-footed tracks. Eventually the way leads to

Willapa Bay and a sandy beach. Listen for the honks of Canada geese and the *"preep preep"* notes of sandpipers. Leadbetter is famous for its thousands of migrating shorebirds and its populations of brant (a migratory black goose resembling a small Canada goose), and snowy plover, which are rare and protected, and are most likely to be found farther north, at the tip of the point. The north half of the Wildlife Area is closed from April 1 to August 31 to protect the snowy plover.

One can either follow the beach back to the starting point or walk northward to the closed boundary of the wildlife refuge. Back on the bay side of the trail, the vista of Willapa Bay on your right will call to your children. The tide flats here contain enough mud to grow hummocks of eelgrass. No matter the season or tide, children will find enough room to run, and countless gulls, ducks, and sandpipers to watch. How many different kinds of sandpipers can your children pick out? (This is a tough challenge: even experts have trouble telling one species of sandpiper from another.) These mud flats have some of the qualities of saltwater life and some of fresh. The birds and plants are unlike those found elsewhere, and give a kind of moonscape feeling.

When you have run out of room to explore, double back and retrace your steps rather than trying to enter the woods and intercept a trail. You may succeed, but it's easy to become confused and lose your way in the pine forest without obvious landmarks.

Forest loop: Of less interest to children but popular with adults is a 1¾-mile forest trail with a ¾-mile road back to the starting point. The 2¼-mile loop begins at the end of the road. First apply insect repellent—remember, bogs breed bugs! From the road end, go left. The trail is wide and made of sand, so children can watch for tracks early in the morning. Angle south, listening to the roar of the breakers, but do *not* be tempted to try to get to the ocean. It is a long way out through sand dunes; many people have gotten lost in the never-never land.

Continue on the loop through shore pine forest on the soft, level trail. Tell children that ocean waves once washed over this place, and that these are old dunes where plants have established themselves and held the sand in place long enough for larger plants to take root. In ¼ mile the trail turns southward. In October and November find wonderful red-and-white-spotted mushrooms, but don't let kids eat them. They are toxic.

A less attractive form of wildlife is the insect world. If you pause very long, mosquitoes and gnats will attack with a vengeance. A good insect repellent, long-sleeved shirts, and long pants will help protect your family. Vegetation becomes more dense, older, and more established the farther south you go. At 1¾ miles reach the road and follow it back to the starting point.

81. Lighthouse Traverse

Type: Dayhike
Difficulty: Moderate for children
Hikable: Year-round
One way: 3½ miles
High point: 250 feet
Elevation loss and gain: 250 feet, 200 feet
Map: Fort Canby State Park brochure

Fort Canby State Park is a popular vacation destination for family vacations. One can easily spend a delightful week, visiting two lighthouses and an interpretive center, making side trips to Oregon and Long Beach, fishing for salmon, playing in the sand, and hiking the three park trails. Leadbetter Point (Hike 80) and Benson Beach (Hike 82) are nearby.

The best-known trail is the 3½-mile Lighthouse Traverse, which takes in the lighthouses at North Head and Cape Disappointment, the Lewis and Clark Interpretive Center, and Fort Canby State Park. As all four destinations can be reached by car, only a determined family out for a challenge will hike the full distance at once. Leave a car at either end or at one of the attractions along the way, or break up the hike into shorter segments for separate outings.

The most interesting segment for children is the ½-mile Discovery Trail from the entrance station of Fort Canby State Park to the Lewis and Clark Interpretive Center. The rewards are thrilling surveys over the Columbia bar, the north jetty, and Fort Canby, and magnificent groves of old-growth Sitka spruce along the way. Children can learn

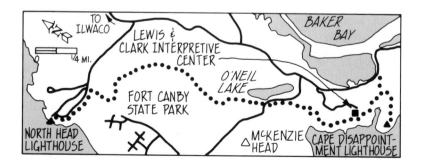

how Captains Vancouver and Meares missed discovering the Columbia River (Meares named it Cape Disappointment because he was so disappointed not to have found the river's mouth), and how Captain Gray discovered the river, named it for his ship, the *Columbia*, and claimed it for America. Share in Captain Gray's thrill at the first view of the river.

Drive to the city of Ilwaco. From the Ilwaco stoplight at First Street and Spruce, follow signs 3.4 miles along a winding road to the entrance of Fort Canby State Park.

A sign will direct you to the road to the North Head lighthouse. Children will find it easy to walk a level ¼ mile to the red-roofed old lighthouse. Explore it freely, then return to the parking lot (elevation 250 feet).

Once there, find a smaller trail marked "Mckenzie Head, 2 Miles," leading down through lush meadow plants. You are actually going to descend only 1¾ miles, to the campground road, instead of to McKenzie Head. (Someone will need to drive the car to the park entrance.) The trail drops steeply through groves of enormous old-growth, barrel-trunked Sitka spruce—some many hundreds of years old. Have children look at the crooks of the trees' bent elbows, which hold clumps of fern. Benches along the muddy descent provide resting points and views out over the Fort Canby campground. The Columbia's north jetty was completed in 1916, and old pictures show that all the land paralleling it where the campground stands today was under water and has filled in since that time. Building the jetty changed the shape of the beach; tell kids, if you are camped in the campground, that the campsite was once under ocean waves, and talk about how the jetty changed the ocean currents.

Continue the descent, passing marshy, lily-pad-covered O'Neil Lake just before exiting onto an unnamed roadbed. Follow it until you reach the paved Fort Canby campground road, turn left, and walk the road for ¼ mile to the gatehouse. This makes a good stopping point or turnaround point.

On the other side of the two-lane road, look for a trail starting upward. This is the Boy Scout–constructed Discovery Trail leading to the Lewis and Clark Interpretive Center. Kids may feel proud to know that other kids built the trail they are walking on. Climb and wind through deciduous second-growth trees on a moss-lined path until the first view at ½ mile. Swallow and catch your breath as you gaze out at freighters from across the Pacific crossing the bar to enter the Columbia. Before the jetty was built, crossing the bar was a much more hazardous affair, as the hundreds of lost ships attest. Listen for ships' bells and the low grumble of their engines. Imagine this view 100 years ago with tall-masted sailing ships, and 200 years ago when it was first discovered and claim was being disputed.

Cape Disappointment Lighthouse

Climb higher on the headland into fields of grass and wild roses sculpted by the wind.

At the interpretive center, at ¾ mile, have children look for World War I gun emplacements, a Lewis and Clark Trail exhibit told in pictures, and dioramas. Directly below the cyclone fence along the cliff, children can see a rookery of nesting black cormorants. Take field glasses so you can look down into their nests. The parking lot below the center is another place you can leave a car for a stopping or turnaround point.

The last ¾ mile of trail leads to the Cape Disappointment light-house, through more enormous old-growth Sitka spruce trees, down a muddy trail, around a fjordlike finger of ocean beach, above the Coast Guard station. (You can also drive to the lighthouse parking area, and walk up an old two-track paved road to the black-roofed Cape Disappointment lighthouse, built in 1916.) From the lighthouse you can look south across the river to the Oregon side and the river's south jetty. In memory of all the sailors and ships lost here, a sign is printed with the poem "Crossing the Bar," by Alfred, Lord Tennyson. If you read it aloud, children can appreciate the poignant significance of the words.

North Head Lighthouse

82. Benson Beach

Type: Dayhike
Difficulty: Easy for children
Hikable: Year-round
One way: 2 miles
High point: Sea level
Elevation gain: None
Map: Fort Canby State Park brochure

This 2-mile-long wide sandy ocean beach calls children to run and chase waves. Unlike other beaches of the Long Beach Peninsula, where vehicles are free to speed along next to waves, this motor-free beach allows families to dig safely in the sand, fly a kite, or just let the children run, unthreatened by cars and off-road vehicles. As tempting bonuses, it has a spectacular headland and rock jetty to explore.

 Drive to Fort Canby State Park, as described for Lighthouse Traverse (Hike 81).

One can reach Benson Beach from any of the park campsites or from the end of the North Jetty parking lot. Wherever you start, walk the beach north to the impressive cliffs below the North Head lighthouse. Backtrack a few hundred feet and take the first trail inland to find a maze of informal paths that weave amongst giant boulders. Look for a cave that surely must have housed Indian families long ago. (More recent users have left pop cans.) Children will want to explore the cave. Ask what was it like to live here in the winter when storms blow waves high into driftwood. These informal trails can also be reached from campsites 161 through 170.

When my children were small we walked out to the end of the

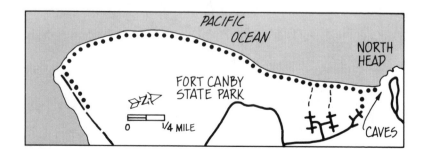

Caves at north end of Benson Beach

jetty. At one time there must have been a roadbed there, but it has collapsed into the rocks with the force of seasons of waves. We scrambled out as far toward the end as we dared, surrounded by crashing breakers on either side. The kids were thrilled by the spray of those waves, and watched as ships and fishing boats disappeared over the horizon. It was a moment to remember forever.

INDEX

About the author:

Seattle resident **Joan Burton** was introduced to hiking as a child, and by the time she had reached her teens, had climbed the six highest mountains in Washington. Later, as a parent with growing children, she introduced not only her own family to the joys of outdooring, but also members of the Girl Scout and Cub Scout groups of which she was a leader. Burton is a longtime member of The Mountaineers, and a graduate of both the basic and intermediate climbing courses taught by that club. A former high school English teacher and author of several magazine articles on outdoor subjects, Burton is now employed at Husky Sports Information at the University of Washington.

Other titles you may enjoy from The Mountaineers:

Best Hikes With Children in Western Washington & the Cascades, Volume 1, Burton.
The first Northwest hiking guide to more than 90 hikes with kid-appeal. Mostly day hikes which also offer camping possibilities; from 1 to 6 miles round trip.

Let's Discover the San Juan Islands, Diamond & Mueller. A children's activity book for ages 6 through 11. Games, puzzles, projects, pictures to color, and more entertain kids and teach them about the area, its wildlife, history, and environmental responsibility.

Nature Walks in and Around Seattle: All-Season Exploring in Parks, Forests and Wetlands, Whitney.
What to see along specific trails of parks and natural areas in greater Seattle. Written for all ages and walking abilities.

Best Hikes With Children in Western and Central Oregon, Henderson.
100 easily-accessible hikes, many lesser-known, with detailed trail information. Tips on hiking with kids, safety, and wilderness ethics.

The **100 Hikes** Series
Best-selling mountain hiking guides, with fully detailed trail descriptions, directions, maps, and photos:

> **Washington's Alpine Lakes,** Spring, Manning & Spring.
> **Washington's North Cascades: Glacier Peak Region,**
> Spring & Manning.
> **Washington's North Cascades: Mount Baker Region,**
> Spring & Manning.
> **Washington's South Cascades and Olympics,** Spring &
> Manning.
> **Inland Northwest,** Landers & Dolphin.

50 Hikes in Mount Rainier National Park, Spring & Manning.

55 Hikes in Central Washington, Spring & Manning.

Mac's Field Guides, MacGowan & Sauskojus.
Two-sided plastic laminated cards with color drawings, common and
scientific names, information on size and habitat:

> ***Northwest Coast Water Birds***
> ***Northwest Coastal Fish***
> ***Northwest Coastal Invertebrates***
> ***Northwest Park/Backyard Birds***
> ***Pacific Northwest Wildflowers***
> ***San Juan Islands***

Animal Tracks of the Pacific Northwest, Stall. Illustrated tracks
and information on 40 to 50 animals common to the region. Available
in book or poster format.

Also in the ***Best Hikes With Children*** series:

> ***Catskills and Hudson River Valley,*** Lewis.
> ***Colorado,*** Keilty.
> ***Connecticut, Massachusetts & Rhode Island,*** Lewis.
> ***New Jersey,*** Zatz.
> ***San Francisco's North Bay,*** McMillon.
> ***San Francisco's South Bay,*** McMillon
> ***Vermont, New Hampshire & Maine,*** Lewis.

Available from your local bookstore or outdoor store, or from The
Mountaineers Books, 1011 SW Klickitat Way, Suite 107, Seattle, WA
98134. Or call for a catalog of over 200 outdoor books: 1-800-553-4453.

The MOUNTAINEERS, founded in 1906, is a non-profit outdoor activity and conservation club, whose mission is "to explore, study, preserve and enjoy the natural beauty of the outdoors...." Based in Seattle, Washington, the club is now the third largest such organization in the United States, with 12,000 members and four branches throughout Washington State.

The Mountaineers sponsors both classes and year-round outdoor activities in the Pacific Northwest, which include hiking, mountain climbing, ski-touring, snowshoeing, bicycling, camping, kayaking and canoeing, nature study, sailing, and adventure travel. The club's conservation division supports environmental causes through educational activities, sponsoring legislation, and presenting informational programs. All club activities are led by skilled, experienced volunteers, who are dedicated to promoting safe and responsible enjoyment and preservation of the outdoors.

The Mountaineers Books, an active, non-profit publishing program of the club, produces guidebooks, instructional texts, historical works, natural history guides, and works on environmental conservation. All books produced by The Mountaineers are aimed at fulfilling the club's mission.

If you would like to participate in these organized outdoor activities or the club's programs, consider a membership in The Mountaineers. For information and an application, write or call The Mountaineers, Club Headquarters, 300 Third Avenue West, Seattle, Washington 98119; (206) 284-6310.